Abortion and Unborn Human Life

Date Due

OC 23 '96			
DE 03 '96			
MY 02 '97			
DE 12 '97			
JA 05 '98			
DE 12 '97			
MR 07 '99			
AG 04 '99			
NO 14 '99			
DE 13 '99			
FE 14 '00			
MR 06 '00			
AP 12 '00			
APR 29 2003			

PATRICK LEE

Abortion and
Unborn Human Life

THE CATHOLIC UNIVERSITY OF AMERICA PRESS

WASHINGTON, D.C.

Copyright © 1996
The Catholic University of America Press
All rights reserved
Printed in the United States of America

The paper used in this publication meets the minimum requirements of American
National Standards for Information Science—Permanence of Paper for Printed Library
materials, ANSI Z39.48-1984.
∞

Library of Congress Cataloging-in-Publication Data
Lee, Patrick, 1952–
    Abortion and unborn human life / by Patrick Lee.
        p.   cm.
    Includes bibliographical references (p.   ) and index.
    (pbk. : alk. paper)
        1. Abortion—Moral and ethical aspects.   I. Title.
HQ767.15.L44   1996
179'.76—dc20
95-34535
ISBN 0-8132-0845-9 (cloth : alk. paper). — ISBN 0-8132-0846-7

Contents

Introduction   1

1. Do Unborn Human Beings
   Become Persons after Birth?   7

2. Do Unborn Human Beings
   Become Persons during Gestation?   46

3. When Do Individual Human Beings
   Come To Be?   69

4. Is Abortion Justified as Nonintentional Killing?   105

5. Consequentialist Arguments   131

Works Cited   157

Index   163

Abortion and Unborn Human Life

Introduction

Several questions arise in the controversy about abortion. Some of these questions pertain primarily to public policy, for example, whether abortion should be illegal, or whether any abortions should be governmentally funded. These questions are distinct from, but obviously related to, the primary moral question: Is the choice to perform an abortion, to procure one, or to help someone procure one, ever morally justified?[1] This last question is the one I am concerned with in this book.

The *prima facie* case against abortion is fairly clear-cut and can be expressed in a simple argument:

Intentionally killing an innocent person always is morally wrong.

Abortion is the intentional killing of an innocent person.

Therefore, abortion is always morally wrong.

---

1. Thus, abortion is not a moral question only for women. In most abortions some man is involved in the choice, a boyfriend, a husband, a father; and often the physician is a man. The moral question is the same whether

I see only three ways of challenging this argument, and therefore only three ways of trying to justify abortion. First, one might deny the second premise, either by denying that what is killed is a person, or by denying that what is killed is even a human being. Arguments that what is killed is not a person are considered in chapters 1 and 2. Arguments that what is killed is not even a human being are considered in chapter 3.

Second, one might deny the second premise by claiming that even if abortion involves killing an innocent person, it is not *intentional* killing and therefore need not be morally wrong. This is the position, in effect, argued for by Judith Jarvis Thomson in her article, "A Defense of Abortion." I discuss this position in chapter 4.

Finally, one might deny the first premise. The standard way of doing this involves consequentialism, that is, one might argue that it is sometimes right to kill an innocent person for the sake of some ulterior end, or for the sake of avoiding bad consequences. I discuss this position in chapter 5.

I will argue that none of the attempts to justify abortion is successful, and that therefore the *prima facie* case against abortion is *ultima facie* sound as well.

In the rest of this introduction I will set out briefly what I take to be the basic evidence which shows that what is killed in abortion is a human person. I will not consider objections in this introduction, but will do that in chapters 1, 2, and 3.

While there are various explanations of *why* intentionally killing innocent human persons is wrong, most people agree that it is morally wrong, at least in most cases, intentionally to kill an innocent adult human being. Most of us also agree that it is wrong intentionally to kill a two-year-old child.

The pro-life argument is that although there are several dif-

---

one is choosing to have one done on oneself, or to help procure, or to perform, the abortion.

ferences between killing a two-year-old child and killing a human embryo or fetus, there is no *morally significant* difference between them. In both cases what is killed is a living, distinct, human individual. As early as eight or ten weeks of gestation—the earliest time at which procured abortions are today performed—the fetus has a fully formed, beating heart; a complete brain (although not all of its synaptic connections are complete); when photographed, is recognizably human to the naked eye; feels pain; cries; and even sucks his or her thumb. Whatever makes killing a two-year-old child morally wrong is equally present in the killing of a human embryo or fetus. Therefore it is wrong intentionally to kill a human embryo or fetus. That is the basic argument, which I shall now go through step-by-step.

1. *The human embryo or fetus is, from conception onward, a distinct individual.* At conception a sex cell of the father, a *sperm,* unites with a sex cell of the mother, an *ovum.* Each of the sex cells contains within its nucleus twenty-three chromosomes, and within the chromosomes are the genes, which contain the information that will guide the development of the new individual resulting from the fusion of the sperm and the ovum. When conception occurs, a sperm unites with an ovum, and the twenty-three chromosomes of the sperm unite with the twenty-three chromosomes of the ovum, so that a new cell is produced that is genetically distinct from the cells either of the mother or of the father. This fusion, or fertilization, is a complicated process, and usually takes seven to ten hours, but at its completion there plainly exists a new, distinct organism.[2]

2. T. V. Daly argues that a distinct organism exists even before the completion of fertilization, at the point of the beginning of syngamy, that is, once the sperm has penetrated the outer wall of the oocyte; see Daly, "Individuals, Syngamy, and the Origin of Human Life: A Reply to Buckle and Dawson," *St. Vincent's Bioethics Center Newsletter* 6, no. 4 (December 1988): 1–7. It seems to me that a functionally distinct organism does not exist until the completion of the fertilization process, when the chromosomes of the two

This new cell, the *zygote,* rapidly begins a continuous process of growth by way of cell division. It divides by twos into two, then four, then eight, and so on. Although in the first few days its cells remain relatively unspecialized, this multicellular organism is a unit and not a mere cluster or colony of cells. The evidence for this point is that without any outside unifying force the cells continue to function as parts of a whole and eventually—certainly by five or six days at the "morula" stage, when its outer cells are specialized for the job of penetrating the mother's uterine wall for implantation—begin differentiated growth. So, with respect to both function and genetic structure, the evidence indicates that after the completion of conception there is a new, distinct, individual organism actively developing within the mother's body.

2. *The embryo or fetus is, from conception onward, human.* Even if the embryo is a distinct individual, this is not logically the same as saying that it is a distinct *human* individual.

The humanity of the embryo is shown by the fact that its sources are two humans, it has the genetic structure that is typical of members of the human species, and its development, barring accidents, ends in a recognizable human individual. It comes from the union of a human sperm and a human ovum. All of its cells are identifiably human, having the typical chromosomal structure. Moreover, the direction of its integrated growth indicates that it is human. It is actively developing itself to the next stage along the maturation process of a human organism.

3. *The human embryo or fetus, from conception onward, is a complete human being.* To say that the embryo is human and individual is not the same as saying that it is a whole human being. If it were human material only apt to function as a *part* of a human organism, then it would not be a human person: a col-

different sex cells have fused and there plainly exists a distinct organism with a functionally united and continuous sequence of events of growth.

ony of human cells in a culture dish, or a beating heart outside the whole human body is human but is not a whole human being.

That the embryo or fetus is a whole human organism rather than functionally a part is shown also by the direction of its growth. Of themselves, parts do not have the ability to develop themselves into the mature stage of the whole organism. But unlike a colony of human cells in a culture dish or a beating human heart outside the body, the embryo or fetus has in itself all of the positive reality and information to develop itself actively into a mature human organism, and so is a whole human being.[3] (Here also lies the essential distinction between a newly formed embryo and a sperm or an ovum.)

4. *Every whole human being is a person.* A person can be defined as an "intelligent and free subject." Every intelligent and free subject is an entity whom we ought to respect, and whose good or fulfillment we ought to will for his or her own sake rather than treat as a mere means. By "intelligent and free subject" is meant, not necessarily someone who is *actually* thinking and willing, but the entity which has the *capacity* to do so. Someone who is asleep or in a coma is a person even though he or she is not actually thinking or willing.

Human embryos have the basic capacities to think and will, even though it will be some time before they exercise those capacities; they are actively developing themselves to the point at which they will perform such acts. Hence all complete human beings, human embryos or fetuses included, are persons.

Moreover, a human person is an intelligent and free, living, organic body. Thus, being an organism is part of what the hu-

---

3. This distinguishes the human embryo or fetus from a hydatidiform mole. The hydatidiform mole is a growth in the womb which arises from incomplete fertilization, so that it is not functionally a whole human being, even though genetically it is human. See Antoine Suarez, "Hydatidiform Moles and Teratomas Confirm the Human Identity of the Preimplantation Embryo," *Journal of Medicine and Philosophy* 15 (1990): 627–35.

man person is, as opposed to a property it has. As a consequence, the organism which a person is cannot come to be or cease to be at a different time than the time at which the person comes to be or ceases to be. For example, *tree* is what this individual thing in my front yard is, whereas its brown color is a property which it has. Its brown color, that is, the brown color of the material that makes up this tree, may have come to be before or after the tree came to be. But since a tree is what the individual is, the individual came to be when the tree which it is came to be, or, expressed differently, when the material that makes up the tree became a tree. Likewise, since *human organism* is not a property which a human person has, but is what he or she is, the time at which the human person comes to be is the same as the time at which the human organism comes to be. Since the human organism comes to be at conception, the human person comes to be at conception also. Hence all human beings, including human embryos or fetuses, are persons.

5. *It is wrong intentionally to kill an innocent human person.* Almost everyone agrees that this is true in most cases, the pro-life position is that it is true in all cases, that it is never morally right to kill an innocent person, even in order to bring about some great benefit or in order to extricate oneself from some terrible problem.

From these points it follows that:

6. *It is wrong intentionally to kill a human embryo or fetus.*[4]

---

4. It is important to point out also that if one is not quite convinced by the arguments which show that what is killed in abortion is a human person, still, the doubt should be resolved on the presumption that what is killed *is* a human person. For if one chooses to kill what may be, for all one knows, a human person, then one consents to killing a human person. This is so even if it should turn out that what is killed is not in fact a human person. What one is morally responsible for is what one chooses, what one consents to. But if one chooses what might be killing a person, then one consents to killing a person.

I

Do Unborn Human Beings Become Persons after Birth?

The position examined in this chapter could be called "the no-person argument." This is the position that, while what is killed in an abortion is a human being, it is not a person and therefore abortion is not morally wrong. Since bearers of rights are called "persons," the same position could be expressed this way: the right to life is not acquired until after birth. The most developed and detailed defense of this position is by Michael Tooley, and so I will refer frequently to his work. Moreover, Tooley's arguments for this position have evolved, partly because of criticism, over a period of several years. Following this history is instructive. Nevertheless, my primary concern is not with Tooley himself but with the general position he has examined and defended in more detail than any other philosopher. In section I, I try to clarify the question whether unborn human beings are persons, and in subsequent sections, I examine the arguments for the position that they are not.

I. "Personhood" and Language

To clarify the question, I first examine what is sometimes put forward as the standard argument in favor of the position that human fetuses *are* persons. It is an argument based on the similarity between successive stages in the development of the fetus in the womb. Roger Wertheimer, in his 1972 article, "Understanding the Abortion Argument," is frequently quoted. Summing up the so-called conservative position, that is, the position that human fetuses are persons and therefore abortion is immoral, Wertheimer writes:

But I am inclined to suppose that the conservative is right, that going back stage by stage from the infant to the zygote one will not find any differences between successive stages significant enough to bear the enormous moral burden of allowing wholesale slaughter at the earlier stage while categorically denying that permission at the next stage.[1]

As a species of slippery slope argument, this argument has its difficulties. Opponents of this pro-life position have pointed out that the fact that differences between *successive* stages in the development of a being are not significant does not show that there are no significant changes at all. There may well be significant differences between *non*-successive stages in the development of the fetus. Thus, Donald Van De Veer writes

More concretely, what impresses many persons who are neither abortionists nor uncomfortably pregnant is that there are substan-

---

1. Roger Wertheimer, "Understanding the Abortion Argument," *The Problem of Abortion,* ed. Joel Feinberg, 2d ed. (Belmont, Cal.: Wadsworth, 1984), 43–44.

tial differences between the early fetal stages . . . and the neonate. Early on, the embryo is quite indeterminately formed, comparatively speaking; in the early fetal stages there is no heart or brain function and no movement of limbs. The empirical differences between what we may loosely designate as S2 or S3 [stage 2 or stage 3] and the neonate are striking.[2]

Analogies clarify the point Van De Veer is making. The difference between sanity and insanity is significant, and yet a person can gradually become insane in such a way that the differences between any two *successive* changes in that person's transformation will be slight.

This point, however, only sharpens the issue. Granted, there are differences, even significant ones, between the zygote and the newborn, but are those differences morally relevant? That is, are they significant in the way the pro-abortion position needs them to be? Are these differences sufficient to ground the differential treatment accorded to newborn babies on the one hand, and embryos or fetuses, on the other hand? When we compare an embryo in very early stages of development with a newborn infant, the differences are marked; yet, there are also important similarities. Van De Veer focuses on the significant differences, but one could also focus on significant similarities. For example, at all stages these beings are of the same species, have human parents, have the same genetic structure, and so on. The real question is: what differences and what similarities are morally relevant? We need a criterion which distinguishes morally relevant differences and similarities from morally irrelevant differences and similarities.

In "On the Moral and Legal Status of Abortion," Mary Anne Warren argues that the human embryo or fetus is human, in the genetic or biological sense, but is not a person. She argues that a fetus lacks those characteristics an entity must have in

2. Donald Van De Veer, "Justifying 'Wholesale Slaughter,'" in Feinberg, *The Problem of Abortion*, 68.

order to be considered a person. She lists the following as required characteristics: consciousness, reasoning, self-motivated activity, the capacity to communicate an indefinite variety of types of messages, and the presence of self-concepts.[3] She says that to be a person an entity need not possess all of these traits, but that it must possess at least some of them. She then says that unborn human beings possess none of these traits and therefore cannot be considered persons.

As evidence for the claim that a thing must have at least some of these characteristics, however, Warren merely asserts that these characteristics belong to the *concept* of personhood: "Furthermore, I think that on reflection even the antiabortionists ought to agree not only that (1)–(5) are central to the concept of personhood, but also that it is a part of this concept that all and only people have full moral rights."[4]

Of course, the claim that unborn human beings possess none of these criteria can be disputed. One could argue that human fetuses satisfy all of those criteria, in that they have the potentiality of exercising the functions referred to in those traits. But the point I wish to make is that the claim that only things which have certain traits are full-fledged members of the moral community is a substantive moral claim. One cannot decide such an issue simply by appealing to the association of traits within a concept in our language community. For no matter what the linguistic conventions of our culture are—although I think, according to those linguistic conventions, an unborn human should be called "a person"—one could always doubt whether those conventions are morally correct. This is not to say that every argument relying on the use of the word or concept *persons* is unsound, but that the claim that unborn humans differ

---

3. Mary Ann Warren, "On the Moral and Legal Status of Abortion," in Feinberg, *The Problem of Abortion,* 102–19. Essentially the same argument is presented by Jane English in "Abortion and the Concept of a Person," *Canadian Journal of Philosophy* 5 (1975): 233–43; reprinted in Feinberg, *The Problem of Abortion,* 151–60.

4. Warren, "On the Moral and Legal Status," 112.

from us in such a way that they lack basic moral rights requires evidence. The argument would have to show, not only that they lack some characteristics associated with entities which have rights, but also why having those characteristics is a necessary condition for having basic moral rights.[5] Most authors who deny the personhood of unborn human beings do not even attempt to establish this crucial step in their argument.

11. Tooley's Early Position

The leading proponent of the position that the right to life is acquired after birth is Michael Tooley. His *Abortion and Infanticide* is an instructive book, even though I disagree with its conclusions. As mentioned earlier, Tooley's argument has undergone some evolution. Earlier versions of his approach were published in 1972 and 1974. We will begin with the earlier and simpler version of 1972, and then observe the argument's evolution up to 1983.

Like Mary Anne Warren and most other contemporary philosophers, Tooley has always granted that the fetus is a human organism.[6] Like Warren also, however, Tooley argues that the right to life belongs to *persons,* and not to every human organism. To have a right to life, he argues, a thing must have certain *psychological* traits.[7]

5. For purposes of the argument in this chapter it does not matter which is primary, rights or duties. I hold, however, that duties are primary, and that things which have rights (persons) are simply those things to whom moral agents have duties.

6. For example: "The first part of the claim [by opponents of abortion] is uncontroversial. A fetus developing inside a human mother is certainly an organism belonging to *homo sapiens*"; from Laura Purdy and Michael Tooley, "Is Abortion Murder?" in *Abortion, Pro and Con,* ed. Robert Perkins (Cambridge, Mass.: Schlenkman, 1974), 140.

7. Michael Tooley, "Abortion and Infanticide," in *Rights and Wrongs of Abortion,* ed. Marshall Cohen, Thomas Nagel, and Thomas Scanlon (Princeton: Princeton University Press, 1974), 57. First published in *Philosophy and Public Affairs* 2 (1972): 37–65.

In his 1972 article, "Abortion and Infanticide," Tooley states his main argument as follows: "An organism possesses a serious right to life only if it possesses the concept of a self as a continuing subject of experiences and other mental states, and believes that it is itself such a continuing entity."[8] He calls this the "self-consciousness requirement." Given this requirement he concludes that since fetuses and infants are not self-conscious and do not have a concept of self, they do not possess a right to life.

To support the first premise of that argument, he argues that there is a conceptual connection between possessing a right to something and having a desire for it. He argues that a right is the sort of thing that can be violated, but a violation can occur only if someone is deprived of something against his desires. Hence one cannot have a right to something unless one desires it; and one cannot desire it unless one has a concept of it. So, to have a right to one's life, one must have a concept of one's life, that is, a concept of an enduring subject of experiences and other mental states.

However, within this article Tooley finds it necessary to modify this simple argument. He notes that there seem to be exceptions to the requirement that a person must desire something in order to have a right to it. He mentions three such cases: an individual may lack a desire to continue to live, for example, because (1) he is emotionally disturbed, or (2) he is temporarily unconscious, or (3) he has been conditioned or indoctrinated not to desire to continue to live. In these types of cases, Tooley notes, most people would say there is a right to life even though there is no actual desire to continue to live.

With these cases in view, Tooley emends his position on rights as follows:

Here it will be sufficient merely to say that, in view of the above, an individual's right to X can be violated not only when he desires X, but also when he *would* now desire X were it not for one of the

8. Ibid., 63.

following: (i) he is in an emotionally unbalanced state; (ii) he is temporarily unconscious; (iii) he has been conditioned to desire the absence of X.[9]

With this criterion for possession of rights, however, he is still able to conclude that fetuses do not have a right to life: "[T]he modification required in the account of the conditions under which an individual's rights can be violated does not undercut my defense of the self-consciousness requirement."[10]

When this 1972 article was reprinted in an anthology published in 1974, Tooley added a postscript, dated June 1973, in which he modified his position further. About the same time, Tooley co-authored with Laura Purdy an article on abortion, and the same amendment appeared in that article.

In his postscript, Tooley writes that one of the modifications introduced within the 1972 article may be, or appears to be, *ad hoc*. He had begun in 1972 by setting out a simple argument: in order to have a right to something, one must have a desire for it. But he then found it necessary to introduce three exceptions: the emotionally unbalanced, the conditioned or indoctrinated, and the temporarily unconscious. He still accepts the exception clauses dealing with the emotionally unbalanced and the conditioned or indoctrinated, for these, he thinks, "are clearly exceptional cases."[11] But he now thinks the exception regarding the temporarily unconscious appears *ad hoc*. And a critic could ask why unborn human beings and infants should not also be considered exceptions. So, he now says that a satisfactory account must make clear the "underlying rationale," that is, the underlying reason why some exceptions should be allowed while others are excluded. The problem can be solved, he says, "by setting out a slightly more subtle account of the conditions under which an individual right can be violated."[12]

9. Ibid.   10. Ibid., 81.
11. Ibid.   12. Ibid.

On the new account, the apparent exception of the temporarily unconscious is handled by referring, not to desires the
individual *would* have, but to actual past or future desires. The
new account is that, except for the emotionally unbalanced and
those conditioned not to desire certain benefits, an action can
violate an individual's right to something only by frustrating
his desire for that thing, generally a present desire, but in some
cases a past or future desire. Thus, the right to life of a temporarily unconscious person is based on his past desire to live.
The rights of future generations, he now adds, are based on
their future desires.

In the 1974 article, co-authored with Laura Purdy, the same
account is set out. In that article the new argument is expressed
as follows: An organism has a right to something only if it has
a desire (either past, present, or future) for that to which it
has a right. One can have a desire, in the morally relevant sense
of "desire," for something only if one has a concept of it.
Therefore, a thing can desire its own continued existence only
if it has the capacity for self-consciousness. The conclusion is
then drawn that since fetuses do not have a capacity for self-
consciousness they do not have a right to life.[13]

Tooley and Purdy conclude that the fetus does not have a
right to life because the fetus is not an actual subject of experiences and other mental states, and does not have a capacity
for self-consciousness. They note that while future generations
have rights based on their future desires, the desires that a thing
would have if it were to live cannot ground a right to life. Thus,
if we knew that there would be no future generations, then we
should not say that it would be wrong to use up all the earth's
resources on the grounds that future generations *would* desire

---

13. In this article they do not argue for a definition of personhood, but
simply state what they mean by the word *person*: "An organism cannot satisfy
this requirement [i.e., of having the desire at some time to continue to exist]
unless it is a person, that is, a continuing subject of experiences and other
mental states, . . ."; Purdy and Tooley, "Is Abortion Murder?" 144.

them *if* they existed. It is only actual desires that count, not desires that entities *would* have under different conditions.[14] On this account, therefore, the desires that a fetus would come to have *if* he or she were not killed are irrelevant.

Up to this point, the argument has been based on the alleged conceptual connection between rights and desires. Tooley has introduced complications into his analysis of rights in order to accommodate various exceptions or apparent exceptions. He began by saying that rights are tied to desires: to violate an individual's right is to deprive him of what he desires. He then added two complications: (1) reference to past and future desires and (2) the exceptions for the emotionally unbalanced and the conditioned or indoctrinated.

iii. Tooley's Later Position

In his 1983 book, *Abortion and Infanticide,* Tooley believes that still more revision is necessary.[15] This time, however, the revision is more drastic. He gives up the claim that there is a conceptual connection between rights and desires. Instead, according to his analysis, rights are based on *interests*. He now argues that an individual may have a right to something based on the fact that it is in his or her interests, regardless of the individual's past, present, or future desires.

The attempt to base the analysis of rights on desires, Tooley now says, must fail because (1) the resulting account will become too complex and (2) it may not be clear when one has arrived at a complete analysis. That is, the alleged conceptual connection between rights and desires becomes quite complex under the pressure of counterexamples. Each new counterexample seems to require yet another revision in one's analysis of a right. But gradually it becomes clear that one could never

14. Ibid., 145.
15. Michael Tooley, *Abortion and Infanticide* (New York: Oxford, 1983).

be sure that new counterexamples would not arise. Hence, basing the analysis of rights on desires must lead to an essentially incomplete, and therefore inconclusive, analysis.

He now says that there is a conceptual connection between interests and rights. He refers to Joel Feinberg's work, agreeing with him on what Feinberg calls the *"interest principle"*: "[T]he sorts of being who *can* have rights are precisely those who have (or can have) interests."[16]

One of the counterexamples which leads Tooley to change his position is that of an individual conditioned or indoctrinated not to desire that to which the individual has a right. For example, a slave is conditioned not to desire his freedom. If rights were conditioned directly on desires, this situation could not involve a violation of any rights. Other counterexamples are a child's right to an education, and a child's right to certain nutrients, say, calcium. Although the child may lack the concepts of a good education and of nutrients such as calcium, and so lack the corresponding desires, the child still has rights to those things. Moreover, simply to posit this type of example as an exception to one's analysis, Tooley now says, is to admit that one has not uncovered the basis of rights as such.

But now it is no longer immediately clear how from his analysis of rights the conclusion can be drawn that fetuses and infants do not have a right to life. For it seems that life is in some sense in the "interest" of the fetus. As he indicates, the old argument (for abortion) cannot be merely patched up.[17]

If rights are based on interests, then why, according to Tooley, do fetuses and infants not have interests? Tooley's answer is that they do have interests—even plants in some sense have interests, he says—but not morally relevant interests. "To be a subject of rights one needs to be capable of having interests in the sense that involves the capacity for having desires."[18] So

16. Ibid., 96.
17. Ibid., 117.
18. Ibid.

although rights are not directly conditional on desires, they are indirectly so insofar as the morally relevant interests are based upon the capacity for having desires. One need not at present possess a capacity to desire the thing to which one has a right, as we have seen. But, failing that, a thing can be in one's interest only if the possession of that thing makes possible the satisfaction of other desires existing at some time in that same individual. So, on Tooley's new analysis, the slave who is conditioned to desire his slavery nevertheless has an interest in freedom because that would make possible the satisfaction of other desires. The individual in a temporary coma has an interest in continued existence on the grounds that his continued existence will make possible the satisfaction of desires existing in that same individual at other times.

But why can't the same thing be said of the continued existence of the fetus or the infant? Tooley's answer is that the fetus and the young child which the fetus becomes are not identical subjects of experience, because the fetus is not a subject of conscious experiences at all.

Thus, Tooley grants that an individual's continued existence can be in his own interest even when he does not have a present desire for his continued existence. But the explanation for this is as follows:

What is needed, apparently, is that the continued existence of the individual will make possible the satisfaction of some desires existing at other times. But not just any desires existing at other times will do. Indeed, . . . it is not even sufficient that they be desires associated with the same physical organism. It is crucial that they be desires that belong to one and the same subject of consciousness.[19]

Tooley then adds the following premise: "Desires existing at different times can belong to a single, continuing subject of consciousness only if that subject of consciousness possesses,

19. Ibid., 120.

at some time, the concept of a continuing self or mental substance."[20] The reason for this is that, according to Tooley, personal identity is constituted by "causal and psychological connections," chiefly by memory. Since the fetus or infant does not have a concept of a continuing self or mental substance, the fetus or infant is not an entity which is identical with a subject of consciousness existing at a later time. And so the continued existence of the fetus or infant does not make possible the satisfaction of desires which exist at another time and which *belong to the same subject of consciousness.* His argument, then, is that the continued existence of the fetus or infant is not in that individual's interest, and therefore the fetus or infant does not have any right to continued existence.

IV. Counterexamples Again

My criticism of Tooley's position will concern, first, his attempt to handle counterexamples; second, how potentialities or capacities bear upon the determination of an entity's moral status; and third, the relationship between consciousness and the physical organism. I set out the first criticism in this section, and the others in subsequent sections. Again, I am concerned not only with Tooley's specific position, but with the general position that the right to life is acquired only after birth (or that the fetus is not a person until after birth), and most specifically, with the position that fetuses do not have a right to life (or are not persons) because they lack some psychological characteristic(s). Hence I will argue against positions Tooley does not hold, or no longer holds, as well as against his actual position.

Tooley underlines the importance of the question of whether potentialities are relevant by comparing the human fetus to nonhuman fetuses, such as a chimpanzee. In the 1974 article

20. Ibid.

co-authored with Laura Purdy, they say that the mental life of a human fetus is not significantly different from that of a non-human fetus such as a chimpanzee. They then conclude that: "Therefore, unless one is prepared to hold that it is seriously wrong to kill nonhuman fetuses, it seems that one cannot maintain that it is seriously wrong to destroy human fetuses."[21] In the next paragraph, Tooley and Purdy say that the proponents of the fetus's rights may still base their argument on the potentiality which the human fetus possesses. However, in this passage they make a significant point: *If one confines oneself to the consideration of what an entity actually does,* then there are no morally relevant differences between the chimpanzee fetus and the human fetus.[22]

Yet in terms of what a thing actually does, a chimpanzee also is not very different from a sleeping person or a person in a temporary coma. If by "mental life" one means actual mental functioning, what one does, then there are several groups of persons who would not qualify for rights on the view that rights are conditioned on actual mental functions, but who surely do have rights: sleeping people, comatose people, and the like. Therefore, the quality of one's *actual* mental state cannot be the decisive feature the lack of which makes fetuses non-persons.

To this the abortion proponent may reply that the sleeping person will, or would, wake up and have desires in the future, and that these desires must somehow be respected. But unless a fetus is killed, he or she will also have desires, just as the sleeping person will unless he or she is killed. So with respect

21. Purdy and Tooley, "Is Abortion Murder?" 141.

22. In *Abortion and Infanticide*, Tooley wants to say that the *potentialities* that a being has are irrelevant to whether it has a right to life now. He distinguishes between potentialities and capacities. Roughly, a potentiality requires a change in the constitution of the thing before the thing can perform the function it has the potentiality for, whereas the capacity does not require such a change, but is immediately exercisable.

to future desires, sleeping people, comatose people, and human fetuses are alike.

Perhaps the difference lies with the past desires of the individual who is asleep or comatose. But here too there is a troubling counterexample. Consider again someone who has been conditioned not to desire that to which he or she has a right. A slave, for example, has been conditioned not to desire his freedom, or a woman has been conditioned not to desire intellectually challenging activity (a charge made by some feminists and mentioned by Tooley). In these cases there are no past desires for the objects the individuals have rights to, but their rights are clearly violated. In fact, this type of case caused Tooley to modify his position in the 1983 book.

Perhaps one might try to explain the difference between the fetus and the other individuals just mentioned (the sleeping persons, the comatose, and the persons conditioned not to desire that to which they have rights) in the following way. The latter individuals have the *capacity* to desire their continued existence, but fetuses do not.

But this view meets other counterexamples. A child has a right to an education, and he has a right to nutrients and vitamins, even though he lacks the concepts of an education and of nutrients and vitamins. Without the concepts of those objects he lacks the capacity, in the sense in which Tooley defines *capacity* (and the only sense in which a fetus would not also have the capacity), to desire those objects. So, it will not do to say that the capacity for desires, in the special sense defined, is the decisive feature the lack of which means fetuses do not have a right to life.

The result is that one cannot say that fetuses lack a right to life either because they lack actual self-consciousness or actual desires (past, present, or future), or because they lack the capacity, defined in the sense Tooley defines it, for having desires.

The case of the slave conditioned not to desire his freedom is instructive. We might compare it to the rights of future generations. In the 1974 article Tooley and Purdy argued that future generations have rights because of the desires they will have; one ought not to frustrate those future desires. But, they added, with the analogous case of fetuses and infants clearly in mind, it is only the desires they actually will have that count, not the desires they *would* have. So, if one discovered there would be no future generations, one should not say it was wrong to use up the world's resources on the ground that they would desire them if they existed. Likewise, according to Tooley and Purdy, killing a fetus also has the result that none of his or her desires will be frustrated.

But surely the judgment regarding the rights of future generations would be quite different if one were contemplating *bringing it about* that there would be no future generations. Clearly, the fact that it is one's own deed that ensures there will be no desires to be frustrated would make a difference. This consideration would not by itself show that any rights of future generations were violated, because persons' rights can be violated only if they actually exist at some time or other, since one cannot violate the "rights" of merely possible entities. On the other hand, this consideration does directly bear on the situation of fetuses and infants, since they actually exist at the time many decisions affecting them are made.

In the relevant respects, fetuses and infants are more similar to slaves who are conditioned not to desire their freedom than to future generations which will never exist. Like individuals who have been conditioned not to desire an object, the only reason why fetuses and infants who are killed will not desire what they lose is that their desires are destroyed along with that which they lose. The key point which the conditioned-slave example shows is that it is irrelevant that a deprivation does not frustrate a victim's desire if (a) the one who deprives the victim of an object he or she would have a desire for is also the one who ensures that those desires will not exist, and (b) the individual who would have such desires does actually exist. The crucial point is that in killing a fetus or an infant one deprives an actual individual of the future life (a life that includes reasoning, self-consciousness, and so on) for which that individual had the potentiality.[23]

v. The Potentiality for Higher Mental Functions

Although Tooley abandoned in 1983 the simple argument that a fetus is not a person because the fetus does not have the capacity for self-consciousness, he still often speaks as though that is his position. More importantly, this position has been defended by others.[24] Thus, it is important to examine this simpler position. Clearly, if "capacity" is construed broadly, then it will follow that unborn embryos or fetuses have the capacity for self-consciousness and other higher mental functions, and thus the position will not constitute a defense of abortion. On the other hand, the proponent of abortion must refer to capacities or potentialities, since no one wants to adopt a position which would justify killing all comatose persons, not to mention sleeping people. So, the denial that fetuses are persons requires distinguishing between the kind of potentiality for mental functions possessed by fetuses and that possessed by comatose or sleeping persons. Then the argument will be that only entities with the second sort of potentiality have a right to life.

Tooley makes such a distinction, calling the first sort "potentialities" and the second sort "capacities." Speaking of capacities, Tooley writes, "To attribute an immediately exercisable capacity to something is to make a statement about how the thing would be behaving, or what properties it would have,

---

23. Cf. Don Marquis, "Why Abortion is Immoral," *Journal of Philosophy* 86 (1989): 183–202.

24. E.g., H. Tristram Englehardt, Jr., "The Ontology of Abortion," *Ethics* 84 (1973–74): 217–34; Warren Quinn, "Abortion: Identity and Loss," *Philosophy and Public Affairs* 13 (1984): 24–54.

if it were now to be in certain circumstances, or in a certain condition."[25] He then contrasts an immediately exercisable capacity with a blocked capacity, that is, a capacity which is joined with "negative factors that prevent the exercise of that capacity."[26] Finally, he contrasts a capacity, in either of the above senses, with a potentiality: "To attribute a certain potentiality to an entity is to say at least that there is a change it could undergo, involving more than the mere elimination of factors blocking the exercise of a capacity, that would result in its having the property it now potentially has."[27] Using Tooley's language, then, we can state the position we are examining in this way: one must have a *capacity* for higher mental functions in order to have a right to life; those entities that have only the potentiality for such acts do not have a right to life.

One weakness of this position, as Tooley later recognized, is that there are counterexamples to it. Unlike the person who is asleep, the person who is in a reversible coma will not exercise consciousness in response to a stimulus. To say that the individual in a coma does have the capacity for self-consciousness, but that it is blocked by the presence of some other positive factor,[28] is simply not true of all persons in reversible comas. Often the brain tissue itself is damaged and requires, perhaps among other things, self-repair. Hence many persons in reversible comas fit the definition of having a mere potentiality for mental acts rather than having a capacity for them, and so constitute a strong counterexample to this position.[29]

A second reason against this position concerns the nature of

25. Tooley, *Abortion and Infanticide,* 149.

26. Ibid., 150.

27. Ibid.

28. This position is adopted by Eike-Henner W. Kluge, *The Practice of Death* (New Haven: Yale University Press, 1975), 91. Tooley discusses this position in *Abortion and Infanticide,* 149.

29. Ronald Cranford, "The Persistent Vegetative State: The Medical Reality (Getting the Facts Straight)," *Hastings Center Report* 18 (1988): 27–28.

potentiality. Embryos or fetuses do have some sort of potentiality for higher mental functions; moreover, the distinction between the kind of potentiality which they have and the kind which they do not have is scarcely as momentous as this position requires it to be. In fact, it is difficult to see why the distinction should be viewed as morally significant at all.

The potentiality for higher mental functions which a human embryo or fetus has is, first of all, an *active* potentiality.[30] Tooley defines "active potentiality" as a condition in which an entity has all of the positive factors necessary for an action, lacking only the appropriate circumstances for its exercise. However, with this definition, one would never have the active potentiality to nourish oneself, or to paint, or to perform any activity that requires outside objects as instruments or material. It is more natural to use the terms "active" and "passive potentialities" to mark the more important distinction between the ability to do something (active potentiality) and the ability to undergo a certain change from another (passive potentiality). For example, the ability of fire to burn is an active potentiality, while the ability of wood to be burnt is a passive potentiality. The ability to walk is an active potentiality, while the ability to be pulled by another body in a gravitational field is a passive potentiality.

The potentialities specific to living things are active potentialities. They are potentialities of an organism to act not on another but on itself; in nourishment, growth, and self-motion, the object of the act, in the sense of what is developed or perfected by the action, is the same as the thing that performs the action. Typically, in such acts some external material is required that is used by the agent in its self-perfective action. In nourishment, for example, the object of the act is the organism itself, and the material used is food.

---

30. Cf. Francis C. Wade, "Potentiality in the Abortion Discussion," *Review of Metaphysics* 29 (1975): 239–55.

The human embryo or fetus is a living being and so has active potentialities that distinguish it from nonliving beings. Now, there is a sense in which the fetus does *not* have an active potentiality to perform higher mental acts. Just as fetuses cannot breathe before they grow lungs, so they cannot perform higher mental acts before their brains develop. But there is also a real and important sense in which the fetus *does* have the active potentiality to perform such acts. The human embryo or fetus is not in the same condition as, say, a canine embryo or fetus. The canine embryo never will perform higher mental acts, and does not have within itself the positive factor required for actively developing itself to the point where it will perform such acts, whereas the human embryo already has that positive factor within himself or herself. The living thing is dynamic, and it has within itself the source of what it will become. True, it needs food, a certain type of atmosphere, and so on. But, given these materials, it actively develops itself to its mature size and structure.

The situation of the human embryo or fetus is this: it is possible that this entity perform a certain action, Z, but to do that he or she must first do X and Y, and he or she is in the process of doing X. Do such entities have the potentiality to do Z or not? I think the answer must be that in one sense they do not, but in another, more fundamental, sense, they do. Nor is this just to say that they *will* have that potentiality. Rather, there is that about them here and now which makes them quite different from other sorts of things which are not actively developing themselves to the point where a more proximate potentiality would be possessed. If one asks, "Does Jane have the potentiality (or capacity) to run a marathon?" it is perfectly natural and accurate to reply, "Yes, after some training she will no doubt succeed." And the point of the reply is that she is now in that sort of condition. Still, if one insists on referring to this positive factor by a different term or phrase, the terminology is unimportant. What matters is that the difference between the kind of potentiality a human embryo or fetus has (not immediately exercisable) and the kind that a sleeping person has (immediately exercisable) cannot carry the moral weight which the proponents of this position load upon it.

Thus, it is true that human embryos or fetuses do not have "capacities" in Tooley's sense, but neither do some people in reversible comas. The difference which Tooley points out between capacities and potentialities seems to have very little moral significance. On the other hand, the distinction between active potentialities (potentialities in a broad sense, so as to include also what Tooley classifies as capacities) and passive potentialities does seem morally significant, at least indirectly, for the following reason. An active potentiality indicates that the entity which possesses it is the same entity as will later exercise that active potentiality. With a passive potentiality that is not so; that is, the actualization of a passive potentiality often produces a completely different thing or substance. The rest of this section explains this point and its application to the rights or personhood of human embryos or fetuses.

First, let us ask why someone would say that higher mental functions or the capacity or potentiality for higher mental functions should be a trait which bestows value on those who have it. There are two possible answers. First, one could say that a capacity for such functions bestows value in the sense that the entities which have such functions and capacities are carriers or recipients for what actually has value. In that case the organisms in which the higher mental functions inhere are not intrinsically valuable, but rather the mental functions and states themselves are valuable and the organisms are only instrumentally valuable. Or, second, one can say that having a potentiality or capacity for higher mental functions (of whatever sort) means that those entities themselves are intrinsically valuable.[31]

31. Robert Nozick discusses these views in *Philosophical Explanation* (Cambridge, Mass.: Harvard University Press, 1981), 453–57.

However, the first view cannot be true. It cannot be that persons are merely vehicles of what really is intrinsically valuable. If that were the case, the basic moral rule would be simply to maximize higher mental functions and states. It would not be morally wrong to kill a child, no matter what age, if doing so enabled one to have two children in the future, to "replace" the one carrier of intrinsic value with two. But this is surely mistaken. So, potentialities for higher mental states are of ethical significance not because they themselves are the only intrinsically valuable entities but because entities which have such potentialities are intrinsically valuable.[32]

If the entity itself is intrinsically valuable, then it must be intrinsically valuable from the moment that it exists. Nothing can come to be at one time but become intrinsically valuable, and hence acquire basic rights, at another time.

Now, when an active potentiality is actualized, the result is the achievement of a higher level of development or perfection by the entity whose potentiality is actualized. Thus, the thing whose active potentiality is actualized continues to exist as a distinct, whole entity. In the actualization of a passive potentiality, however, often the result is that the entity, or some components of the entity, enters into the constitution of a distinct, larger entity, and so the original entity no longer exists after the change.

In the relevant case, when the sperm and the ovum fuse to become a zygote, which is a distinct organism, the sperm and the ovum do not survive as distinct and whole entities. Rather, the genetic material in each enters into the constitution of the larger entity, the new organism which comes to be through their fusion. Thus, a sperm has no active potentiality to develop any of the traits of mature human beings; it has only the passive potentiality to surrender its material into the constitution of a

32. Cf. Philip E. Devine, "The Moral Basis of Vegetarianism," in *Moral Dilemmas: Readings in Ethics and Social Philosophy,* ed. Richard L. Purtill (Belmont, Cal.: Wadsworth, 1985), 389–96.

human being. Stated otherwise, the sperm and the ovum simply have no potentiality to become mature human beings, or to perform activities specific to human beings, because they do not survive past the fertilization process. But the zygote, the new embryo, is a distinct organism which actively develops itself in a continuous fashion until it reaches the mature stage of its development, a mature human being. Thus, the fact that it has the active potentiality for the traits of a mature human being means that the actualization of its potentiality does not produce a distinct entity, but rather the maturation of the same entity which existed since conception. Since this entity is identical with the entity a few years later which indisputably is intrinsically valuable, consistency demands that one hold that this entity now is intrinsically valuable.[33]

33. When thinking of "capacities" or potentialities one often thinks of such capacities as the ability to run a six-minute mile, to play a musical instrument, to work mathematical problems, or the like. Such abilities, however, are quite different from the more basic potentialities, such as the abilities to move, to grow, to see, to reason, and so on. In the Aristotelian tradition the former were called *habitus* and the latter were classified as natural active potentialities. The distinction is important. The ability to run a six-minute mile and the ability to play the piano are refinements, or specifications, of the basic potentiality to move. They are acquired by repeated acts; the repeated acts in some manner dispose the agent so that its potentiality is more specific or perfected in relation to the dispositions to exercise an already existing potentiality in a particular way. The other potentialities, on the other hand, are not acquired by repeated action. When are these potentialities—to grow, to nourish oneself, to sense, to reason—acquired?

Because the specific dispositions are produced by repeated action, they come to be only with the repeated action. But the source of the natural active potentialities is the thing itself. There is then a sense in which the natural active potentialities come to be when the thing in which the active potentialities inhere comes to be. And here it is important to recall the contrast of the active potentiality with a passive one. (The passive potentiality might very well come to be with the coming to be of the thing itself also. But, with the passive potentiality there is no temptation to treat the thing which already has the passive potentiality as equal in worth with the end result of the actualization of the passive potentiality. The actualization of a passive potentiality may produce an entirely different thing.)

In sum, the distinction between capacities and potentialities which Tooley emphasizes lacks moral significance. The distinction between active and passive potentialities, however, is morally significant, because the possession of an active potentiality for consciousness indicates that the thing which has such a potentiality is identical with the thing which will later exercise that potentiality, something not true of entities which have merely passive potentialities.

VI. Desires and the Embryo or Fetus

As we have seen, at one time Tooley held the position just criticized, but abandoned it before his 1983 book. In *Abortion and Infanticide,* he holds that for the right to life, the capacity for self-consciousness is not necessary, but that it is necessary to be a subject of nonmomentary interests. Tooley acknowledges that some individuals who lack a capacity for self-consciousness nevertheless have a right to life. And he also concedes that individuals, for example, those indoctrinated not to desire something, can have a right to something without having desired it. So, he now holds that an individual can have a right to its continued existence *either* if it now desires to continue to exist, *or* if its continued existence will make possible the satisfaction of desires which exist in it at other times.[34]

Tooley argues, however, that in human beings the subject of consciousness which later has desires is not, contrary to what one might think, the same subject as the embryo or fetus which exists in the womb. He holds this because he also claims that there must be *psychological continuity,* especially memory links, among desires and among other mental states for there to be an identical subject of consciousness existing over time.[35] Since

34. Tooley, *Abortion and Infanticide,* 121.
35. Ibid., 117–20.

there are no memory links between the embryo or fetus, on the one hand, and the individual at a later age, on the other hand, Tooley holds that the desires that later come to be do not belong to "one and the same subject of consciousness."[36]

I will criticize the possible bases for this position in the next section. In this section I criticize his claim concerning how desires and rights are connected. Consider again the case of the slave who is conditioned not to desire his freedom. If Tooley's position on desires and interests were correct, that would mean that the enslavement was wrong because it made impossible the satisfaction of other desires which belong to the enslaved individual. But why should the fact that enslavement frustrates desires for things *other* than freedom or lack of enslavement be the explanation of the essential wrong in this case? Doesn't that misplace the violation? Isn't the deprivation of freedom *in itself* a violation of rights, independently of whether it leads to the frustration of other desires? This point is clear again in the case of a woman conditioned not to desire intellectually challenging activities (another example discussed by Tooley). Suppose that being deprived of such activities did not frustrate any other desire for any other object. Still, the deprivation would in itself harm that woman and violate her rights.

Hence the connection between desires and rights which Tooley tries to retain is misconceived. It seems more reasonable to hold that the violation of someone's rights is more closely connected with what truly *harms* the individual than with what he or she desires. A human being is a definite type of thing. Some conditions or activities truly perfect a human being while other conditions truly—that is, independently of what you or I might think—diminish a human being. For example, knowledge, life, health, and friendship truly perfect human beings. Ignorance, death, sickness, aloneness truly diminish a human being.[37] (Of course, a certain degree of autonomy is also a real

36. Ibid., 118–21; 130–46.
37. For more on this, see Germain Grisez and Joseph Boyle, *Life and Death*

benefit for a person, and so desires often are relevant, but secondarily, as a component in autonomy.) If this is true, then the decisive question is whether a person is harmed or deprived of a real benefit (something which is really fulfilling for them) or not. One cannot, then, use the alleged connection between rights and desires, at least in the manner Tooley does, as a way of establishing the extension of rights.

VII. Dualism

The second way in which one may argue that human beings do not acquire rights until after birth is to deny that the person is a physical organism. There are two ways of doing this. First, one may argue that the person is a nonphysical subject. Tooley seems to take this position in 1983. Second, one might deny that the person is a subject at all, maintaining instead that the person is simply a series of experiences. I will examine the first position in this section and the second in the next.

As we saw earlier, Tooley later rejected the position examined in section V, that the fetus is not a person because the fetus does not have the capacity for self-consciousness. Yet he maintained in his 1983 book that personhood is acquired after birth. The reason why the fetus lacks a right to life, Tooley says, is not simply that he or she lacks a capacity for self-consciousness, for he concedes that an individual can lack such a capacity but have a right to life.[38] Rather, he claims there is no identity between the fetus and any later subject of consciousness.

---

with Liberty and Justice (Notre Dame: University of Notre Dame Press, 1978), 336–80.

38. Tooley, *Abortion and Infanticide*, 118–21; 130–46. A temporarily comatose individual without a capacity for self-consciousness (because of very severe but reparable brain damage) has a right to life, according to Tooley, because his or her continued existence will make possible the satisfaction of desires which will belong to this same subject of consciousness. But the same cannot be said about the unborn human being, because, he says, in the very

Tooley holds that a comatose individual has a right to life because his continued existence would make possible the satisfaction of his or her desires existing at other times. Tooley considers whether something similar might not be said of an embryo or fetus:

Let Mary be an individual who enjoys a happy life. Then, although some philosophers have expressed doubts about this, it might very well be said that it was certainly in Mary's interest that a certain embryo was not destroyed several years earlier. This claim, together with the tendency to use expressions such as 'Mary before she was born,' to refer to the embryo in question, may lead one to think that it was in the embryo's interest not to be destroyed.[39]

But Tooley rejects this suggestion, arguing that it rests on a conceptual confusion. If one is talking about the very early embryo before she has consciousness, then Tooley gives the following reason for rejecting it: "A subject of interests, in the relevant sense of 'interest', must necessarily be a subject of conscious states, including experiences and desires."[40] Nor can Mary be identified with the baby from which she grew. If Mary were able to remember experiences the baby enjoyed, and thus there were causal and psychological connections between the baby and Mary, then the identification indeed could be made. But memories do not extend back to the preborn stage. And Tooley's claim is that such psychological connections, apparently chiefly those of memory, are necessary for personal identity. Without such connections there is not an identity of subjects of consciousness:

On the other hand, suppose that not only does Mary, at a much later time, not remember any of the baby's experiences, but the experiences in question are not psychologically linked, either by

---

early stages of gestation the fetus is not a subject of consciousness at all, and even in the later stages, it is not an *enduring* subject of consciousness.

39. Ibid., 118.
40. Ibid., 118–19.

memory or in any other way, to mental states enjoyed by the human organism in question at *any* later time. Here it seems to me clearly incorrect to say that Mary and the baby are one and the same subject of consciousness, and therefore it cannot be correct to transfer, from Mary to the baby, Mary's interest in the baby's not having been destroyed.[41]

Now, if the organism persists throughout time, but the subject of consciousness does not exist throughout that whole time, then either the subject of consciousness is distinct from the organism (dualism), which seems to be what Tooley is supposing, or there is no subject, but the person is the experiences themselves standing in a certain unity (the "no-subject view," which will be discussed in the next section). Such are the positions on the subject of consciousness to which this view leads.

Tooley seems to presuppose a dualist position at several points in his argument where he discusses cases of "reprogramming" individuals, that is, replacing the memories and personality of one individual with that of another. According to him, such "reprogramming" destroys a person, who is a subject of experiences, although it does not destroy a physical organism.[42] The assumption is that the person is a subject of experiences and other mental states *associated with* a physical organism, but not identical with the physical organism.

It is difficult to show that dualism is mistaken. In a way, the mistake is so massive that it is difficult to articulate the overwhelming evidence against it. First of all, strong evidence against dualism exists in the vast amount of data showing a close correlation between functions of the brain and mental functions. While one can reject dualism without saying that in every type of conscious act these functions are identical, dualism has no adequate explanation of this correlation. If the person is a nonphysical subject, why do the person's operations so

41. Ibid., 119–20.
42. Ibid., 97–103, 118–20.

closely depend on physical states? Dualists have never provided a plausible answer to this question. In fact, dualists who have tried to give an account of the relation between cognitional mental functions and physical states have tended to end in skepticism.

Looked at more closely, however, the phenomena involved in perception provide material for a cogent case against dualism. I will present the argument in four steps. The first step points out that it is the same "I" which understands and which senses or perceives. That is, it is not one thing which performs the act of understanding and a distinct thing which performs the act of perceiving. It is the self-same agent which performs both actions.

This important first step in the argument must be fully understood. Those who hold that the human person is a subject or thing distinct from the human physical organism hold, of course, that the person is that which understands, and that which is conscious. This first point recognizes that the thing referred to as the source of understanding and self-consciousness is identical with the thing which perceives.

Evidence for this point can be found by analyzing singular judgments. When I affirm, for example, that *That is a tree,* it is by my understanding, or an intellectual act, that I apprehend what is meant by "tree" and apprehend objects as unitary, living things. Viewing such an affirmation or judgment as having a subject-predicate structure, we can say that the predicate of the judgment expressed here is grasped by my understanding. However, the subject of the judgment, what I refer to by the word "that," is apprehended by perception. What I mean by "that" is precisely that which is perceptually present to me. But, clearly, it must be the same thing which apprehends the predicate and the subject of a unitary judgment. So, it is the same thing, the same agent, which understands and which perceives.

The second point is this. Perceiving is a bodily act. This is not to say that it is performed by "a mere body," as opposed to a soul. Rather, while understanding may be a spiritual act, that is, an act not performed by a bodily organ (whether that is so is not important for our topic, and so we abstract from that question), perception is an act performed by a physical organism by means of a bodily organ.

This point sets aside the theory of perception held by Descartes, among others.[43] Descartes, for example, held that sensation or perception is a purely mental event. There is some change, of course, in the body which is a prerequisite to the act of perceiving, a change in the eyes, or the ears, or, in updated versions of Descartes' theory, a change in the neurons; but the act itself of perceiving is a conscious act performed not by the body but by the consciousness associated with the body. Neither the body, nor any part of the body, shares in the act itself of sensation or perception.

This view of sensation or perception is highly implausible. As well as being aware of our own acts of perception—upon which Descartes and other dualists understandably focus—we arrive at the concepts of sensation and perception in the first place in order to account for the activities animals perform which are not performed by plants. In the life and activities of an animal, perception is a component in a larger action which consists in the animal's adaptation to his environment. We can see this clearly if we observe a dog chasing a rabbit. The dog zigs this way and then zags that way in what is clearly an effort to catch his prey. The zigging and zagging are actions which are specified by the dog's perception of the present position of the rabbit. The whole group of activities clearly has a unity, and the unity is a particular way an organism adapts to its singular, material environment. The dog's perception of the rabbit is just a component in that larger adaptation of the dog to his

---

43. See also Richard Swinburne, *The Evolution of the Soul* (Oxford: Clarendon, 1986), 21–62.

environment. So, since the adaptation as a whole is a bodily, organic activity, it follows that the sensation or perception is also a bodily, organic activity.[44]

Of course, human beings do not normally chase rabbits. But human beings sometimes do chase dogs. And the chasing of a dog by a human is clearly the same sort of activity as the dog's chasing of a rabbit. Hence the argument which showed that the dog's sensation or perception is bodily applies equally to the sensation or perception performed by a human being.

That perception is a bodily activity has also been amply demonstrated by Maurice Merleau-Ponty in his monumental *Phenomenology of Perception*. Merleau-Ponty's analyses show that the dualist conception of the ego as a pure consciousness making use of the body simply does not fit with the data. Perception is far different from a purely mental act, observing, as a spectator, the changes produced in the body. Rather, perception is a function of the body-subject's interaction with his or her world. Already on the pre-conscious or prereflexive level, the body as an organism relates to various objects in one's environment insofar as they are possible terms of one's bodily actions.[45] What one perceives, then, is a world seen as a correlate of what one can do. Up and down, near and far, the various shapes perceived, are perceived as they are partly because of the body-subject's "dialogue" with the world. The body itself, he shows, actively organizes its field of vision. The world we perceive originates in a bodily project. Thus, the body is already a subject, already in "dialogue" with the world, on the pre-conscious level. Therefore, perception is neither a purely mechanistic phenomenon, nor a purely mental act of a consciousness which is a subject distinct from the body. Perception is a

44. On this argument as a whole, see also David Braine, *The Human Person: Animal and Spirit* (Notre Dame: University of Notre Dame Press, 1992), esp. 290–341.

45. Maurice Merleau-Ponty, *The Phenomenology of Perception*, trans. Colin Smith (New York: Routledge and Kegan Paul, 1962).

psycho-physical act, the deepest levels of which lie below self-consciousness on the organic level.

The third step is to draw a conclusion implied by the previous point. If sensing or perceiving is a bodily, organic activity, it follows that what does the sensing or perceiving is a bodily thing, that is, an organism. We learn what type of thing we are dealing with by learning what types of activities it performs. Various things are distinguished precisely by their different types of actions and reactions. Thus, a thing which performs organic activities must be an organism.

The fourth step is the conclusion implied by the first and third steps. If that which understands and is self-conscious is identical with that which senses or perceives, and that which senses or perceives is a physical organism, it follows that that which understands and is self-conscious—what dualists themselves refer to by the word "I"—is a physical organism.

We see then the argument presented by Michael Tooley and others that, although the fetus is a human organism, it is not a person because it is not conscious, is mistaken. This argument identifies the person as a subject of consciousness or experience, a subject that is somehow associated with the human organism but is other than it. But since the human person is essentially an organism, one cannot hold that the human organism comes to be at one time while the person comes to be at a later time.

VIII. The No-Subject View

A second way of denying that a human person is a physical organism, a physical subject, is to deny that the person is a subject at all. On this view, articulated by such thinkers as David Hume, Williams James, and Bertrand Russell, the person is a string or series of experiences rather than a subject or substance underlying experiences. Although what Tooley actually says seems to imply a dualist position, it is difficult to believe he wants to embrace that position; more likely, he would opt for a no-subject view. This view has been made popular again recently by some proponents of the position that personal identity consists in psychological continuity.[46]

A clear expression of this position can be found in Russell's lectures on *The Philosophy of Logical Atomism*. He argues there that there is no need to suppose that the various experiences of a person are united by the fact that they all inhere in a persisting substance. Rather, there must be some empirical relation among those experiences which moves us to associate them when we reidentify the person. Now, whatever that relation is, we can define the person simply as the series of experiences which have that relation to one another, and can then dispense with the unnecessary supposition of an underlying, and unexperienced, ego or self. As Russell puts it:

Therefore we shall say that a person is a certain series of experiences. We shall not deny that there may be a metaphysical ego. We shall merely say that it is a question that does not concern us in any way, because it is a matter about which we know nothing and can know nothing, and therefore it obviously cannot be a thing that comes into science in any way. What we know is this string of experiences that makes up a person, and that is put together by means of certain empirically given relations such, e.g., as memory.[47]

Now, if this were the correct view of the self, then one could argue quite straightforwardly that since a person is a string of experiences united by memory, the string does not begin until there is an experience of which some later experience is a memory. Perhaps, though, inclusion in memory is not the only way later experiences are related to earlier ones such that both are ex-

---

46. Cf. Peter McInerney, "Does a Fetus Already Have a Future-Like-Ours?" *Journal of Philosophy* 87 (1990): 264–68; and Derek Parfit, *Reasons and Persons* (Oxford: Oxford University Press, 1984).

47. Bertrand Russell, *The Philosophy of Logical Atomism,* ed. David Pears (La Salle, Ill.: Open Court, 1985), 150.

periences of a single person. Perhaps continuity of beliefs, character, and intentions also play a role. In any case, on the view we are examining, the person is a series of experiences which have certain psychological relations or continuities among them, and those relations or continuities do not extend to the early stages of the life of the embryo or fetus, and perhaps they do not even extend to the early life of the infant.[48] Therefore on this view the embryo or fetus, and perhaps also the young infant, is not a person.

Much of the discussion on this issue of personal identity, as opposed to the more traditional question of how the mind relates to the body, concerns what to say about imagined cases of transference of brains, "body-swapping," and the like. The question in such discussions is: what are the necessary and/or sufficient conditions for person A at one time being the same person as person B at a later time? Must B have the same brain as A? Must B have the same memory as A did? Could the memories, beliefs, character, and intentions of A be transferred to B's body and, if so, would B then be the same person as A even though he would now have a totally different body?

Considering such questions is certainly not idle, but, just as in considering imagined cases in ethical discussions, one must be careful not to beg important questions by assuming that everyone's intuitions about what to say of a given scenario will be the same.

Considerations about imagined cases can sometimes show, or at least suggest, that a theory cannot be defended as coherent. I believe that the reduplication objection to the psychological continuity theory of personal identity does just this. Suppose we say that personal identity consists in (rather than simply is evidenced by) continuities of beliefs, memory, character, and basic intentions. In other words, person A is identical with person B if person B has the same beliefs, memories,

48. Cf. McInerney, "Does a Fetus Already Have a Future-Like-Ours?"

character, and basic intentions as person A—even though person A and person B (at different times) have different and non-continuous bodies. Then, as Derek Parfit points out, it would be possible in theory for someone to invent a machine called a "Teletransporter," which would transfer *me,* that is, according to this view, my memories, character, intentions, and so on, to a completely different body. It would be possible for me to "teletransport" to Mars in a matter of minutes. When I entered such a machine, says Parfit:

The Scanner here on earth will destroy my brain and body, while recording exact states of all my cells. It will then transport this information by radio. Traveling at the speed of light, the message will take three minutes to reach the Replicator on Mars. This will then create, out of new matter, a brain and a body exactly like mine. It will be in this body that I shall wake up.[49]

But suppose the teletransporter makes not one but *two* copies of my brain. The two copies go to live in two different cities, developing therefore different beliefs and at least slightly different characters, memories, and intentions. Both have the psychological continuity with me such that, on the basis of the psychological continuity view, each is I. Yet, after a time, they have significantly different properties, and so they cannot be identical with each other. Nor are there different respects of identity in question here, so that one could say that one of the offshoots is identical to me in one respect but different in a different respect. The reduplication objection concludes that it is more reasonable to hold that in the imagined teletransporter case the teletransporter makes *replicas* of the original self rather than literally transporting the self. And the argument is that since the psychological continuity theory of personal identity leads to a self-contradiction, it must be false. That is, call the first copy A and the second B. On the psychological continuity

49. Cf. W. R. Carter, *The Elements of Metaphysics* (New York: McGraw-Hill, 1990), 94; and Parfit, *Reasons and Persons,* 199.

view, A is identical to me, and B is identical to me, and, by the transitivity of identity, it follows that A is identical to B. But since A now has different properties from B it also follows that A is not identical to B. Hence the psychological continuity view of personal identity leads to a self-contradiction, and so must be false.

Attempts to avoid this difficulty seem to me *ad hoc*. One can simply give up the idea of numerical personal *identity*, or one can stipulate that only the *closest* psychological continuer is identical with me, but these moves seem to me to deny truths we are more certain of than what such moves are trying to save.

Secondly, the same argument which shows that the human person is a physical organism also shows that the self cannot be a mere series of experiences. The position that human beings or other animals are things or substances which persist throughout time is not an a priori necessary truth. It is not logically inconceivable that we could have a world with entities which do not persist at all. The evidence that there are persisting substances, and that human beings and other animals are persisting substances, consists in all of the phenomena which show beyond reasonable doubt that human beings and other animals are *agents,* and that they remain the same sort of agents, and numerically the same agents, throughout long stretches of time. The actions initiated and sustained by animals—chasing prey, eating meals, mating—are actions which take time. To suppose that there are only experiences strung together in various ways is to lose sight of the fact that in countless cases an action and its structure is explained by the kind of agent that produced and sustained it. A dog will chase a rabbit, whereas a horse will not. This is partly because a dog is a carnivore while a horse is a herbivore. But this is most reasonably interpreted as meaning that a dog is a certain type of agent, that is, a persistent source of predictable actions and reactions: given certain circumstances, this type of agent will act or react in certain ways.

When talking to another person it seems clear that it is the same entity, the same thing, which sees the movement of his lips and his expressions and hears what he says. In turn this thing seems to be the same thing which talks to him, and which is seen and heard by him. In other words, the person is a bodily subject which persists through time, and what I refer to as "I" is the same thing which other people refer to as "he" or "him," namely, a certain type of living, breathing, walking, talking, thinking thing, that is, a certain type of organism.

Again, there seems to be a consciousness of the unity of oneself when one is conscious of oneself as an agent. When I deliberate about whether to go jogging or to stay home and study, I am trying to determine which of two incompatible activities I will perform. I begin the process with a desire to jog and also with a desire to study. I am aware that both of these desires cannot be satisfied. Moreover, I am also aware that I must now determine which desire (if either) I will now act on. Now, what I am aware of here is that the thing which acts is not a mere effect of the competition between incompatible desires, but an agent which is not a different entity, *cannot* be a different entity, from the entity which has these various desires. But this is an entity which persists through time. Therefore, what I am directly aware of entails that I persist through time, rather than being a series of experiences or events.

Russell argued that whatever the experienced relation was that led one to posit an underlying substance, one could manage by positing only that relation. However, this point simply ignores the explanatory value of the nature of the agent. One loses explanatory power by denying what one seems to understand, namely, the unity of the diverse actions of the one thing.

Once again, what applies to other agents, in particular, to other animals, applies also to human beings. A human being is a certain type of agent, which means that, given certain circumstances, it will act or react in certain ways. (For example, if told a joke, a mature human being will often laugh; not so with other animals.) That there are agents which persist through time and that human beings are among them, is apprehended by insight into sensory data, and is amply justified by the explanatory force of such an understanding.

As we have seen, there are three ways of holding that a human being becomes a person or acquires the right to life only after birth. One way, criticized in section V, is to say that (1) the human physical organism is, eventually, the subject of those capacities or acts which confer rights, but (2) the human organism comes to be at one time, but acquires rights only when it acquires the capacity for higher mental acts (as opposed to the potentiality for them). Against that position I argued that there are counterexamples and that the distinction between capacities and potentialities cannot be of such moral significance as this position claims. This argument showed that the thing which has basic rights acquires them whenever it comes to be.

In the second position that holds that a human being acquires the right to life after birth, one might grant that the distinction between potentialities and capacities is not the crucial point, and one might grant that the thing which has basic rights has them as soon as it comes to be, but one holds that the basic rights belong to a subject of consciousness distinct from the human physical organism. This is the position I criticized in section VII. That criticism showed that the human person is identical with the human physical organism.

The third way of holding that a human being acquires the right to life after birth is to deny that a person is a subject which persists through time, and thus to deny that a human person is essentially a physical organism which comes to be when the human, physical organism comes to be. Against this I argued in section VIII that human action can be accounted for only by holding that the person is a persistent subject of various actions and events.

Gathering these points together, one can say the following:

(1) the thing which has basic rights acquires them at the time at which it comes to be; and (2) the thing which has basic rights is the human organism. I shall argue in chapter 3 that (3) the time at which the human organism comes to be is conception. Therefore, the conclusion will follow: human beings acquire basic rights at conception.

A different way of expressing the argument is as follows. It is agreed that killing adult human organisms is (at least *prima facie*) wrong. To determine whether killing unborn human organisms is wrong, one need only determine what feature of killing adult human organisms makes doing so wrong, and then determine whether that feature is also present in the killing of unborn human organisms. In this chapter I have examined three proposed features. First, some hold that killing adult human organisms is wrong because they have a capacity, not to be confused with a mere potentiality, for higher mental functioning. I argued against this position (a) that the distinction between capacities and potentialities is not morally significant, as the argument requires, and (b) that the capacities or potentialities of a thing are important because they show that the thing itself is (or is not) intrinsically valuable, and so the time that the thing with the relevant capacities or potentialities comes to be is also the time that it begins to be intrinsically valuable.

Secondly, some hold that killing adult human organisms is wrong because the continued existence of those organisms is a means for the realization of higher mental functions by subjects of consciousness associated with those physical organisms. Against this position I argued that the subject of consciousness *is* the human organism.

Thirdly, some hold that killing adult human organisms is wrong because it harms, or frustrates the desires of, a person, and by "person" is meant a series of experiences connected by various psychological relations. Against this I argued that this view would imply that persons could be duplicated, and that this implication conflicts with basic facts about a person which we know to be true, namely, that a person existing at one time cannot be identical with two different persons existing at a later time. I also argued that persisting, unitary actions can best be understood as performed by a persisting agent.

2

Do Unborn Human Beings
Become Persons during Gestation?

In the last chapter I criticized the position that the human organism becomes a person only after birth. Its proponents grant that every person has full moral rights, but they require some developed psychological capacity in a thing for it to be classified as a person. In this chapter I examine and criticize the position that the fetus becomes a person some time between conception and birth. Usually, proponents of this position also hold that the fetus only gradually becomes a full person, that is, that there are degrees of personhood or moral standing. So, according to this view, while late abortions are wrong, early abortions are not wrong at all and the later an abortion is, the closer it is to being wrong or the more seriously wrong it is.

The position examined in this chapter has important distinctive features. Whereas most of the proponents of the position examined in chapter 1 concede that one either is or is not a person, with full moral rights, proponents of the position considered in this chapter hold that there are degrees of personhood and hence degrees of moral standing. As a consequence, this position has a distinctive rhetorical appeal.

1. The Gradualist Position

According to the view we are examining, there are varying degrees of moral standing, such that very young embryos have none at all, somewhat older embryos or fetuses have some but not full moral standing, and older fetuses have approximately the same moral standing as infants. So, according to this position, early abortions are permissible but late abortions usually are not. This view is presented as a moderate position, as the golden mean between the extremes of the conservative and the liberal positions regarding abortion. I will use L. W. Sumner's *Abortion and Moral Theory* as representative of this position.[1] Other proponents are S. I. Benn, Norman Gillespie, and Bonnie Steinbock.[2]

According to Sumner, both the conservative and the liberal views have insuperable difficulties. He argues that the liberal view cannot consistently distinguish between abortion and infanticide, and that the conservative view cannot consistently distinguish between abortion and contraception. The difficul-

1. L. W. Sumner, *Abortion and Moral Theory* (Princeton: Princeton University Press, 1981). Part of this has been reprinted and revised as L. W. Sumner, "A Third Way," in *The Problem of Abortion,* ed. Joel Feinberg, 2d ed. (Belmont, Cal.: Wadsworth, 1984), 71–93.

2. S. I. Benn, "Abortion, Infanticide, and Respect for Persons," in Feinberg, *The Problem of Abortion,* 135–44; Norman Gillespie, "Abortion and Human Rights," in Feinberg, *The Problem of Abortion,* 94–101; and Bonnie Steinbock, *Life Before Birth: The Moral and Legal Status of Embryos and Fetuses* (New York: Oxford University Press, 1992).

ties of the liberal and conservative views stem, according to Sumner, from a common source. Both make the mistake of holding that all fetuses, regardless of age and development, have the same moral standing. To remedy this defect, Sumner proposes his "third way," according to which the moral standing of a fetus varies according to its age and development.[3]

To determine whether a thing has moral standing, and if so, how much, one needs a *criterion* of moral standing. The criterion Sumner proposes is sentience. Sumner presents two arguments to support this criterion. First, Sumner argues that only by using this criterion does one arrive at judgments on the key moral issues that cohere well with our basic moral intuitions. In his view it "coheres better than either of its predecessors with our considered moral judgments both on abortion and on cognate issues."[4]

The second argument is based on the notion of harm or benefit, that is, what meets or opposes a person's interests. What counts as a benefit or a harm is either the fact that the person's desires are satisfied or frustrated, or the fact that the person is brought to experience what he likes or dislikes. From this premise Sumner concludes that benefits and harms for particular persons must be psychological states and that morality, which concerns harms and benefits, "can concern itself only with beings who are conscious or sentient."[5] Since *sentience* is the criterion of moral standing, it follows that all sentient beings, all animals, have some degree of moral standing.

According to Sumner, the degrees of moral standing correspond to the degrees of sentience among various animals. "The animal kingdom presents us with a hierarchy of sentience. Non-sentient beings have no moral standing; among sentient beings the more developed have greater standing than the less developed, the upper limit being occupied by the paradigm of

3. L. W. Sumner, "A Third Way," 71.
4. Ibid., 72.
5. Ibid.

a normal adult human being."[6] According to Sumner, it is a great merit of this theory that "it seems to accord reasonably well with most people's intuitions that in our moral reasoning paramecia and horseflies count for nothing, dogs and cats count for something, chimpanzees and dolphins count for more, and human beings count for most of all."[7]

With this criterion, Sumner concludes that the fetus has no moral standing at all in the first trimester of gestation, since in that period he or she is presentient; that this organism begins to acquire moral standing in the second trimester; and that the moral standing of the fetus in the third trimester is equal to the moral standing of a newborn infant. He thus holds that abortion in the early stages of pregnancy is no different than contraception, while abortion in the later stages of pregnancy may have a moral quality approaching that of infanticide. Sumner favorably describes this view of the status of the fetus as "gradual, differential, and developmental."[8] He believes this approach accords much better with our commonsense intuitions.

The rhetorical appeal of this approach should not be underestimated. Any position which can be presented as taking a virtuous mean, especially on a highly controversial issue, has tremendous appeal. People naturally fear outright confrontation and so a moderate position—which allows one to say that one partly agrees with each side without, of course, their alleged peculiar exaggerations—has significant appeal.

---

6. Ibid., 83. Again: "As the duties may vary in strength, so may the corresponding rights. To have some moral standing is to have some right to life, whether or not it may be overridden by the rights of others. To have full moral standing is to have the strongest right to life possessed by anyone, the right to life of a paradigm person" (ibid., 74).

7. Ibid., 84.

8. Ibid., 73.

II. Against Sentience as the Criterion of Moral Standing

There are two difficulties with this position. First, there is a difficulty in holding that sentience is the criterion of moral standing. Secondly, there is a difficulty in how that criterion is applied. The second difficulty is more central. For, even if sentience were the criterion, it would still not follow that human embryos or fetuses have any less moral standing than infants or adults. I will discuss this difficulty in the next section. Nevertheless, I believe it is important to see also that sentience is not the true criterion of moral standing. If one holds that sentience is the criterion of moral standing, and therefore that all animals have moral worth or moral rights, then there is a strong psychological pressure to admit degrees of moral standing or worth. It is difficult even for trained philosophers to maintain that a cockroach, which is a sentient being, has the same degree of moral standing as a human being. So in this section I argue against the position that sentience is the criterion of moral standing.

There seem to be only two reasons why one would hold that whatever has sentience has some degree of moral standing. First, we tend to think of the "self" as what has feelings. "Feelings" would include our emotions and our sensations, especially pleasure and pain. We naturally tend to have affection for those things which are like us in some way. Thus, our affections, the emotional level of ourselves, tend to empathize with all other things which in any way have sentience and thus feelings. This natural empathy can make it seem that our general concern or love should extend to all animals, not just to those who happen to be of our species, or to those species which are rational.

Such feelings by themselves, however, can no more be an argument for a moral position than can feelings of aggression toward others who seem to threaten us or feelings of sexual desire. The data recounted in the last paragraph become material for a properly ethical position only when, partly on their basis, one identifies what is to be protected and pursued with what can be felt, that is, enjoyed or suffered, in some way. In other words, this first basis for holding that sentience should be the criterion of moral standing is a hedonist position. If what is intrinsically good is what can be enjoyed, and the intrinsically bad is suffering, then it is not incoherent to hold that sentience is the criterion of moral standing. That, at least, is one possible basis for this position. (It is not the one offered by Sumner— his position will be discussed in a moment.)

Hedonism has serious difficulties. In 1974 Robert Nozick and Germain Grisez with Russell Shaw independently introduced a thought-experiment about an "experience machine."[9] This thought-experiment helps to show that any position which identifies value or goodness with conscious experience, or a quality of conscious experience, is mistaken. Nozick writes:

Suppose there were an experience machine that would give you any experience you desired. Super-duper neuropsychologists could stimulate your brain so that you would think and feel you were writing a great novel, or making a friend, or reading an interesting book. All the time you would be floating in a tank, with electrodes attached to your brain. Should you plug into this machine for life, preprogramming your life's experiences?[10]

Most of us would choose not to plug into the experience machine. And this point shows that we care about something other than the mere experience of activities: we see that the reality of which we can have experience is inherently worthwhile. The very fact that we can choose an option other than the one offering a life replete with positive experiences shows

9. Robert Nozick, *Anarchy, State and Utopia* (New York: Basic Books, 1974), 42–45; Germain Grisez and Russell Shaw, *Beyond the New Morality*, 3d ed. (Notre Dame: University of Notre Dame Press, 1988), 35–37 (the first edition was published in 1974).

10. Robert Nozick, *Anarchy, State and Utopia*, 42.

that what is intrinsically valuable is not experience alone. For we can choose one option over another, or even hesitate about one option in comparison with others, only if that option offers something which the other options do not offer. As Nozick points out, the thought-experiment shows that we care about actually *doing* certain things, and actually *being* in certain ways, as opposed to the mere experience of doing or being in certain ways.[11]

Moreover, as Grisez and Shaw argue, to identify goodness or value with conscious experience is to locate the good in only one part of the self, consciousness.[12] But the person is more than consciousness, as we showed in chapter 1. Thus, we cannot identify value or goodness as enjoyment or satisfaction of conscious interests. But the identification of what is good and worthwhile with conscious experience or an aspect of it is one basis for adopting sentience as the criterion of moral standing. So, if the other basis for that adoption is also mistaken, this will show at least that the position has serious difficulties.

The second possible reason for holding that sentience is the criterion for moral standing is the one set out by Sumner. As we saw, Sumner holds as evident that what is good, what should be protected and pursued, is what is in our *interest*. But an interest, he says, is the object of a desire or preference. Thus, only those who can have desires, hence those who have sentience, can have interests; and all those who have desires and sentience have interests. This position identifies the good, not with conscious enjoyment, but with the satisfaction of desires or preferences (sometimes called "antiperfectionism," although sometimes "perfectionism" and "antiperfectionism" are terms having political meanings).

Difficulties with this position begin to emerge when one considers desires based on mistaken beliefs and desires for ob-

---

11. Ibid.
12. Grisez and Shaw, *Beyond the New Morality*, 35–36.

jects which are clearly harmful to the one who desires. To handle such problematic desires one must refer not to just any desires or preferences but to *informed* preferences. One is then faced with the difficulty of specifying what to count as a sufficiently informed desire or preference.

But these are just symptomatic of the fundamental flaw in this position. In any of its variants it holds that what makes a thing good is the fact that it is desired (or would be desired). And this is to put things backwards. For it is still possible to ask: "But what is it about these objects, as opposed to those, which makes them such that we should, or even can, desire them?" Clearly, it is not purely arbitrary which things human beings desire, any more than it is arbitrary which things horses or tigers desire. What, then, in the objects desired distinguishes them from other objects not desired? Such questions show that it is not just a question of which came first, the desire or that in the object which makes it worthy to be desired. Since our desires are not purely arbitrary (which is not to say there cannot be disagreements and mistakes about them), it follows that prior to being desired, the object desired has about it something which makes it fit to be desired. Thus, what makes a thing good cannot consist in its being the satisfaction of desires or preferences; rather, desires and preferences are rational only if they are in line with what is genuinely good.

We deliberate about what to do because we recognize that there is some point in acting and that not all courses of action would equally realize what we see as worth pursuing. We recognize some reason or reasons for acting, because we experience various activities and then understand in some of them that they are fitting to us, that the realization of such possibilities would be perfective or good. Thus, what makes something intrinsically valuable cannot be merely that it satisfies desires or preferences; rather, it must be objectively fitting or fulfilling of human persons. The good is what is really perfective of us. We should want this or that, but our wanting them is not what makes them good.[13] So, the position which identifies what is good with what happens to satisfy desires or preferences cannot reasonably be used to argue against the rights of fetuses, or the severely retarded, or so on. This point does not show where we should draw the line between things whose perfection we should desire, and things which we can use and whose intrinsic perfection we need not respect. But it does show that the interest theory, at least as understood in such a way as to exclude unborn human beings from full moral standing, is without rational foundation.

III. Against Degrees of Moral Standing

Even if the criterion of moral standing were sentience, nevertheless, we would still have to conclude that human embryos and fetuses have full moral standing.[14] As I pointed out in the last chapter, there are two ways one may apply a criterion of moral standing. One might hold that the criterion indicates the states or qualities that are valuable and should be maximized or even respected. Or one might hold, on the contrary, that the criterion is some property or nature such that all of the entities which have that property or nature have moral worth. Suppose sentience *were* the criterion of moral worth. In the first way of applying the criterion one holds, in effect, that the states of sentience are valuable, and the moral rule will be that they should be maximized and for that reason alone things which have sentience or can have those states should, generally, not be

13. Cf. Germain Grisez and Joseph Boyle, *Life and Death with Liberty and Justice* (Notre Dame: University of Notre Dame Press, 1978), 336–80.

14. So, the argument in section II was not *logically* necessary. Nevertheless, it may have been *psychologically* necessary. Even though it does not follow logically that if sentience is the criterion for moral standing, then there are degrees of moral standing and then one can argue that embryos and fetuses have only partial moral standing, still, psychologically, it is difficult to hold that all animals have the same moral worth. Thus the argument in section II is needed.

killed. In the second way of applying that criterion, however, one holds that the entities themselves are intrinsically valuable or have intrinsic dignity. Then, what has intrinsic value is not just the state of sentience, in its varying degrees of richness, but the sentient beings themselves.

This is an important difference. On the first view, the physical organisms which are sentient are not intrinsically valuable, but are only the vehicles or perhaps the recipients of what really has intrinsic value. On the second view, the organisms themselves are intrinsically valuable.

The second way of applying the criterion of moral worth—whatever that criterion turns out to be—must be correct. If the first view were correct, it would follow that the basic moral rule would be simply to maximize those valuable states or functions. It would not be morally wrong to kill a child, no matter what age, if doing so enabled one to have two children in the future, and thus to bring it about that there were two vehicles of intrinsic value rather than one. On the contrary, we are aware that persons themselves, which are things enduring through time,[15] are intrinsically valuable.

But if the thing itself is intrinsically valuable, then it is intrinsically valuable from the time it begins to be, not just when it acquires a state or property such as sentience.[16] If X is in itself valuable, apart from any further features or relations not already included in just being X, then as soon as X comes to be, X must be intrinsically valuable: it cannot come to be at one time, and become intrinsically valuable at another time. So, even if sentience were the criterion of moral worth, it would remain true that human embryos or fetuses have intrinsic worth, because they are identical with entities who at a later time possess actual sentience.

The same point can be shown in another way. If what is good

15. See chap. I, sect. VIII.
16. See chap. I, sect. V.

or beneficial does not consist in a conscious experience, then in what does it consist? The example of the experience machine suggests that a good or benefit is simply a reality which is really fulfilling. As argued above, the beginning of thinking about what to do is grounded in the recognition that those possible actions which perfect us would be good to do or pursue. We desire things not only because they are pleasant, but often primarily because they are (or seem) fulfilling or perfective. We desire various activities for their own sakes: knowledge, friendship, technical excellence ("doing a job right"), health, and so on. The only feature these activities have in common is that they are, in different ways, fulfilling or perfective of us or of others we care for.[17] (We desire fulfillment not only for ourselves but for others as well—we are not by nature egoists.)

Now, if the fulfillment of a thing is intrinsically good, then the thing itself, and not just its properties, must also be intrinsically good. For the fulfillment of a thing is not entirely distinct from the thing itself, but is its full-being. To use Aristotelian terminology, while accidents are distinct from the substance, it is precisely the substance itself that is actualized or perfected in its accidents. Thus, if what is intrinsically good is real fulfillment or perfection, then, whatever the entities are in whom inherent value or good can inhere, they themselves, as well as their full flourishing, are intrinsically valuable. It is incoherent to hold that the fulfillment of a thing is intrinsically valuable, but that the thing itself is not.

It follows that the gradualist position is mistaken. If we consider a healthy human adult, the paradigm case, some say, of someone who has a right to life, then that human being is intrinsically valuable, and not just that person's experiences. But, as I argued in chapter 1, the human being is essentially an organism. Therefore, the time at which the human organism

17. Cf. Germain Grisez, Joseph Boyle, and John Finnis, "Practical Principles, Moral Truth, and Ultimate Ends," *American Journal of Jurisprudence* 32 (1987): 99–151, esp. 100–111, 133–35.

comes to be is the time at which the human being comes to be. So, if Jones is a human being, then Jones came to be when the human organism which Jones is came to be.

Let us add the following moral proposition. If X is intrinsically valuable, and it is wrong directly to kill X at a certain time, then, other things being equal, it is also wrong directly to kill X at some previous time. So, if it is wrong directly to kill a human being today, then, other things being equal, it would have been wrong directly to kill that human being at any previous time. In particular, since the human being is essentially a physical organism, and the organism comes to be at conception (which will be shown in chapter 3), then it is wrong to kill a human being whether he or she is two years outside the womb, or one month past conception, or three days past conception.

The same point can be made in still another way. Speaking about distributive justice in general, Alan Gewirth proposes a proportionality principle. Gewirth writes, "The logical form of that proportionality is: if *x* units of some property Q justify that one have *x* units of some right or duty E, then *y* units of Q justify that one have *y* units of E."[18] Norman Gillespie, adopting this principle, argues that the characteristics which are relevant to determining moral standing will therefore be comparative, and so adults will have more of whatever the relevant characteristic is than fetuses or embryos do.[19]

This position would make sense only if the criterion of moral standing were a quality or property. However, the criterion of moral standing is not a property which things *have*, but *being an instance of a certain type of thing*. And this characteristic, by the nature of the case, is *not* comparative. One either is or is not an instance of a certain type of thing. One either is or is not a human being, or an intelligent and free agent (which, I

18. Quoted by Norman Gillespie, "Abortion and Human Rights," in Feinberg, *The Problem of Abortion,* 95.
19. Ibid.

will argue in the next section, is the correct criterion of moral worth).[20] Gewirth's principle is applicable in many instances of distributive justice, but it cannot be applied to the primary question of which subjects should be treated with justice.

Finally, it should be noted that, while proponents of the grad-ualist position seldom apply their position to other groups of human individuals, if it were correct, it would logically apply to others as well. The differences among degrees of moral standing could not be confined to the unborn and infants. Already-born people differ in their capacities and qualities, and so some would be "more equal" than others. Thus, the re-tarded, the insane, the handicapped, and other groups would have to be "re-evaluated."[21]

Thus, Sumner and other proponents of the gradualist posi-tion apply the criterion of moral standing in the wrong way, because they fail to see that the criterion should be used to pick out the *things* which have intrinsic value rather than the states or properties one should maximize. The same point can be ex-pressed differently: They have placed the criterion of moral standing in the wrong category. The criterion must be in the category of things rather than properties or qualities.

IV. The Criterion of Personhood

If sentience is not the criterion of personhood or moral worth, then what is? Being a member of the human species is not a *necessary* condition for having moral standing (although, I will argue, it is a *sufficient* condition). If intelligent life from another planet landed on earth, we would owe them moral re-spect also.

As explained above, when we reason about what we will do or ought to do, we recognize some activities as being good and

---

20. In Aristotelian terms, there are no degrees in the category of sub-stance. And persons, I argue, are particular types of substances.

21. Cf. Grisez and Boyle, *Life and Death,* 233–34.

fulfilling and thus as activities to be pursued. That is, we begin to act, and deliberate about acting, because we understand that it would be good to realize certain possibilities. Such activities constitute our ultimate reasons for acting. And, as I argued in section II, these ultimate reasons for acting are not types of enjoyment or pleasure, but are aspects of our real fulfillment. Now, we recognize such activities or basic goods as worth pursuing not just for ourselves, but for others as well. When I understand that learning is a good, for example, I understand it as perfective for anyone who can realize such a good.

In other words, I see these objects as good not just for me, but for others like me. But in some way or other I am like everything else in the universe. The question is, what is the relevant likeness? The activities in question are objects of practical reason and choice, that is, they are possibilities for a rational, free agent. Such objects are in fact fulfilling for the thing which I am: a rational agent, a human being, an animal, an organism, and so on. But they are understood not precisely as fulfilling in these other ways, but as fulfilling for a rational agent, as answering the question of what I should rationally pursue. This is not to say that they are good only when pursued by reason and choice, for my life is good even while I am sleeping and knowledge is good even when reached spontaneously and not by choice. But in these beginnings of practical or moral reasoning, I apprehend, not that life in general is good, but that the sort of life that can be an object of free and rational pursuit is an intrinsic good.[22] And so, those to whom I can will these goods are those for whom such objects *can* be good, and they would be only rational and free agents. Thus, the criterion of personhood or moral standing is *being a rational, free agent.*

This criterion can be defended in the following way. Non-rational animals are more similar to other sorts of beings than

22. Cf. Grisez, Boyle, and Finnis, "Practical Principles, Moral Truth, and Ultimate Ends," 102–13.

they are to persons. As far as we can determine, nonhuman animals lack free choice. The cause of their actions is wholly exterior, that is, the kind of stimulus put before them completely determines which actions they perform. Thus, which goals their actions will be directed to is determined by others. In this sense they are like slaves: someone else, necessarily, selects their goals for them. They are, by the nature of the case, instruments. Free agents, on the other hand, have the capacity to select their own goals.[23] We should treat things in accordance with the way they are. Therefore, we should not treat free agents as mere things; we should not use them as mere means, without taking account of their own good. But since other animals are not free agents, it is not treating them unduly to direct them to our ends, that is, to use them as mere means, be it for food, for work, or otherwise.[24]

To say that the goods of rational and free agents generate moral responsibilities is to refer to rational and free agents as concrete things or substances. Thus, children before they actually reason and comatose or very senile human beings are rational and free agents. Moreover, the goods which one must pursue and respect are fundamentally aspects of what persons *can be*; that is, they are various potentialities or possibilities to which persons are naturally oriented. Therefore, a person, a being with full moral standing, comes to be when a thing which has these basic potentialities comes to be.

A rational and free agent is a thing which has the potentiality to pursue the various personal goods rationally or freely. Since human persons are organisms, they come to be at conception, and from that moment on they have the active potentiality to realize all of the fulfillments of a human being, although it may

23. Cf. Thomas Aquinas, *Summa contra gentiles*, book 3, chapter 112; and the prologue to *Summa theologiae*, Part I–II.

24. This is not to say that we have a right to exploit the environment any way we see fit. Although the environment does not have rights, still, as the home of present and future generations, and as God's creation, God's art, it demands a type of respect.

take them some time to actualize those potentialities. Human embryos and fetuses are rational and free agents because they are identical with the things which at a later time reason and freely choose, and they are actively developing themselves to the point where they will perform such acts. The important point for morality is that life, knowledge, friendship, and so on, are possibilities or potentialities for *this very being* even though it may take this being many years to actualize those potentialities. Indeed, these beings are even now *actively developing* themselves to the point at which they will realize these perfections.

Finally, the point is not that they *potentially* have those characteristics which confer personhood. To have such characteristics only potentially would mean that they have personhood only potentially. Nor is the point that they are potential persons and therefore have rights. Rather, being a thing which has the potentiality rationally to pursue these various goods is what confers *actual* personhood, and human embryos and fetuses have that characteristic actually, not just potentially.

Why, someone might object, should having the same potentiality as adult human beings give embryos, fetuses, and infants the same moral status as adults? Should not what a thing *does* actually, count more than that for which it has the potentiality? Why should we be concerned so much with potentiality? The answer—and I think it is very important for this controversy over abortion—is that our actions, our choices, primarily bear upon potentialities, on what can or could be. If I kill someone, I do not, strictly speaking, take away from them their actuality. It is too late to deprive them of what they have been or what they are. My action, rather, deprives them of what they could have been, it brings it about that they will never actualize their remaining possibilities. In other words, it is too late to deprive them of their past or present; if I kill them, what I deprive them of is their future.[25] And so our actions and our choices bear

25. Cf. Don Marquis, "Why Abortion is Immoral," *Journal of Philosophy* 86 (1989): 183–202.

primarily upon potentialities. Therefore, killing an unborn child is, in this respect, worse than killing an adult, because it deprives him or her of even more of life than the adult.

v. Derivative or Detached Objection?

Ronald Dworkin's influential 1993 work on abortion is primarily concerned with the legal issue, although he does have a chapter entitled, "The Morality of Abortion." However, the book is important for our purposes because if its main argument is accepted, it would follow that any serious moral or legal objection to abortion must be based on a religious or quasi-religious position and therefore would be quite inadmissible as a proposal for influencing public policy. Although I do not wish to delve into the legal issue of abortion in this book, still, it is worth asking how the overall argument against abortion set forth here is related to Dworkin's account of the issue. Does this argument depend on religious premises, as Dworkin claims all, or the vast majority of, antiabortion arguments do, or is it, as I claimed in the introduction, a strictly philosophical argument, one that can be accepted by people of almost any religious faith, or of no religious faith at all?

Dworkin argues that when people object to abortion, arguing that abortion is murder or homicide or an assault on human life, they could mean two very different things. First, they could mean that human embryos or fetuses are entities which have interests in staying alive and therefore have a right to life which is violated by abortion. This he calls the "derivative" objection, because in this case one's objection to abortion is derived from a recognition of their rights. On the other hand, one might mean that human embryos or fetuses have intrinsic value and that abortion is wrong because it destroys something which is sacred or valuable. This he calls the "detached" objection, because it does not depend on any rights or interests.[26]

---

26. Ronald Dworkin, *Life's Dominion: An Argument About Abortion, Euthanasia, and Individual Freedom* (New York: Random House, 1993), 11.

Similarly, one might strenuously object to the destruction of great art, not because it violates the rights of those pieces of art, but because something of intrinsic value would be destroyed. People who object to abortion on detached grounds believe that it is a "kind of cosmic shame"[27] when any human life is destroyed, but not that in abortion someone with interests and rights has been deprived of his or her rights.

Dworkin argues that, despite their language and what they often say, hardly anyone really objects to abortion on the basis of a derivative objection. The objection of almost all opponents of abortion is actually a detached objection. His evidence is that the public opinion polls show that, while many do indeed object to abortion, many of those who do so also think it should not always be illegal. Likewise, many of those who think abortion is wrong still think there are various exceptions where it is morally right and also should be legal, such as in cases of rape or incest, or, for a smaller portion of the public, when the child would be severely retarded.[28] But if a fetus is really thought to be a human person with interests and rights, just as you and I have interests and rights, it would be sheer inconsistency to hold that the government should not protect this being, or that it is permissible to kill this being if he or she was conceived in rape or incest, or if he or she will be retarded. Dworkin concludes that the great battle over abortion (and the great battle over euthanasia) is about "the intrinsic, cosmic value of a human life," rather than about the rights of fetuses.[29] This allows him to argue, subsequently, that since the objections people have to abortion are really of a religious or quasi-religious nature, having to do with one's basic metaphysics or world-view, attempts to make abortion illegal are attempts to impose one's own religious or quasi-religious world-view on others and to limit their constitutionally protected liberties to do so.[30]

27. Ibid., 13.
29. Ibid., 15.

28. Ibid., 13–16.
30. Ibid., 102–17.

The evidence Dworkin presents to support his claim that the vast majority of opponents of abortion actually have a detached objection rather than a derivative objection is flawed. In effect, Dworkin is claiming that people cannot be opposed to abortion on the grounds that fetuses are persons, since most people do not draw all of the warranted conclusions from that premise: many of them hold that abortion is permissible in cases of rape or incest or likely severe retardation of the child; many of them hold that abortion, while morally wrong, should not be against the law. But, in the first place, this ignores the point that many opponents of abortion do hold consistent positions on these issues: many do hold that it is immoral even in cases of rape, incest, and the child's likely retardation, and many hold that it should be against the law in all cases except where the mother's life is at stake.

Moreover, Dworkin simply ignores the possible role of prejudice or unjust discrimination in the formation of people's opinions. In the 1850s many people did hold that one should not kill slaves or mistreat them, but still saw nothing wrong with owning them. In the 1950s most Americans did think it was wrong to kill African Americans, even though many saw nothing wrong with excluding them from jobs, good schools, and so on. In other words, although both in the 1850s and in the 1950s many Americans did hold that African Americans were persons, they were far from drawing all of the appropriate conclusions from that truth. But if Dworkin's argument were sound, by the same logic one could have argued that the objections of Americans to killing African Americans had to be detached objections. Moreover, if abolitionists were not prepared to allow African Americans equal participation in society—and few were—then one could also have argued that the abolitionist case was an attempt to impose religious views on the rest of us, in particular, against the Southern slave-owners whose liberty was being infringed.

I would argue, against Dworkin's hypothesis, that what prevents some opponents of abortion from holding that abortion is wrong in cases of rape and incest is, not that they do not truly think the fetus is a person, but that this truth has not registered for them as it should, due to prejudice. Likewise, some hold that abortion is morally wrong, but that it should not be illegal. Dworkin is quite right that this position is inconsistent if their objection is a derived objection. Dworkin argues that they must be consistent and therefore their objection is the detached rather than the derived objection. However, if human fetuses really are persons with rights—which is the position I argue for—it would be quite surprising if people *were* entirely consistent in their attitude to these persons whose care is sometimes viewed as quite burdensome. Just as many people knew that African Americans are persons and yet, because of prejudice, did not fully appreciate their personhood, the same is true for unborn human beings.

What does Dworkin say of the *derived* objection to abortion, that is, the position that human fetuses really are persons who have interests and rights? He claims that it simply makes no sense,[31] and that it is a "scarcely comprehensible idea."[32] His argument is, a thing has rights only if it has interests that can be violated; and a thing has interests only if it has or has had some form of consciousness. "It makes no sense to suppose that a thing has interests of *its own*—as distinct from its being important what happens to it—unless it has, or has had, some form of consciousness: some mental as well as physical life."[33] Dworkin concedes that there is an entity in the womb for whom the abortion might be thought to be bad. He insists, however, that one cannot coherently say that it is against the fetus's interests to be aborted. We have seen this argument before, but Dworkin goes further, considering possible objections. Dworkin argues that the fact that the fetus is en route to

31. Ibid., 16.   32. Ibid.
33. Ibid.

becoming a full human being is not enough to say that the fetus now has interests: "Imagine that, just as Dr. Frankenstein reached for the lever that would bring life to the assemblage of body parts on his laboratory table, someone appalled at the experiment smashed the apparatus. That act, whatever we think of it, would not have been harmful or unfair to the assemblage, or against its interests."[34] Dworkin then notes that one might object that, unlike the body parts on Dr. Frankenstein's table, the fetus is growing toward the status of a mature human being, with no outside help. To this Dworkin replies that there is outside help, either from the mother or from scientific ingenuity.[35] And, finally, he says that all of these points are irrelevant because the clearest point is that a thing can have interests only if it has, or has had, consciousness.

However, Dworkin offers not the slightest argument for this contention. His dismissal of the position that human fetuses do have interests and rights is offered without support. The outside help from the mother or the scientist for the human embryo or fetus to which Dworkin refers is help in the form of sustenance and assistance for the intrinsically organized growth of a unitary organism. As I show in the next chapter, the biological evidence indicates that the human embryo or fetus is an actively developing, unitary organism, identical with the organism that will later be born, identical with the organism that will later walk, identical with the organism that will later talk, and so on.

The analogy with the body parts of the Dr. Frankenstein's monster is misleading. The human embryo or fetus is an actively developing organism, identical with the organism that will later perform all of the actions typical of mature members of the human species. The body parts on the table, however, are more analogous to the sperm and the ovum: the constitu-

34. Ibid.
35. Ibid.

ents of these entities (the wood and metal on the table, the chromosomes in the sperm and ovum) will enter into the make-up of another entity, but they are not identical with the later, living entities.

Dworkin's position is that the object of a right is the satisfaction of a conscious preference. That is, he identifies the good with the satisfaction of conscious desires. For this reason, those who lack consciousness are without rights. I have already tried to show that this position is mistaken. I argued in section II that to identify the good with the satisfaction of conscious preferences is to deny that our preferences are rational only if they are for what is genuinely good; what is genuinely good grounds our preferences, rather than vice versa. So, on the one hand, Dworkin gives no argument for his position, apparently thinking that its fit with various examples suffices to recommend it; on the other hand, there are, as argued above in section III, insuperable difficulties for this theory of the good and the criterion of moral standing.

Is the position defended here in this book, then, a detached objection or a derived one? It is clear that it is a derived objection. My argument is that human embryos and fetuses are subjects of rights and that it is wrong to kill them, for the same reason it is wrong to kill any human being. This argument does not at any point appeal to theological or religious premises.

In sum, the gradualist position is that the embryo or fetus gradually acquires moral standing, that early abortions are no different than contraception and are morally permissible, but that late abortions approach the seriousness of infanticide and are generally wrong. I have argued that, first, the only reason one could have to support the criterion of moral standing this view supposes is the identification of what makes a thing good with conscious experience or the satisfaction of preferences, and that those positions are mistaken. Secondly, I argued that even if sentience were the criterion of moral standing, as proponents of this view hold, it would not follow that early embryos or fetuses have no moral standing, because, when correctly applied, the criterion of moral standing picks out things which have intrinsic moral standing, and they have that moral standing from the moment they come to be, not just when they actually have the relevant desirable property or state in its fullness. Thirdly, I argued that what makes good things good is, not a quality or type of experience, but real fulfillment, a point that provides further support to the position that certain things themselves, as opposed to just their states or properties, are intrinsically valuable and are so from the time they come to be. Fourthly, I argued that the criterion of moral standing is being a rational and free agent. Since this is a type of thing or substance, it does not admit of degrees, and human embryos or fetuses meet this standard from the time they come to be. Finally, I clarified the relationship between the argument presented in this book and Ronald Dworkin's claim that almost all objections to abortion are based not on the rights of the unborn, but on their sacredness or intrinsic value. They are indeed intrinsically valuable, but in such a way as to possess rights.

3

When Do Individual Human Beings Come to Be?

Having argued in chapter 2 that human beings are intrinsically valuable from the time that they come to be and in chapter 1 that, since they are essentially physical organisms, human beings come to be at the time at which the human physical organism comes to be, in this chapter I address the question: When does the human organism come to be? I will argue that the human organism comes to be at conception, that is, fertilization. I will first indicate in section I why biologists usually place the beginning of a new human individual's life at fertilization, and in subsequent sections I will discuss opposing views. The critical examination of these arguments will help to clarify and strengthen the argument that a new human organism begins at fertilization.

The majority of biologists who discuss fertilization and gestation of the embryo place the beginning of a new individual human being at fertilization. Here are some examples:

The formation, maturation and meeting of a male and female sex cell are all preliminary to their actual union into a combined cell, or zygote, which definitely marks the beginning of a new individual. This penetration of the ovum by spermatozoon, and the coming together and pooling of their respective nuclei, constitutes the process of fertilization.[1]

Zygote. This cell is the beginning of a human being. It results from the fertilization of an ovum by a sperm. The expression "fertilized ovum" refers to the zygote.[2]

Embryonic life commences with fertilization, and hence the beginning of that process may be taken as the *point de depart* of stage I.[3]

These pronuclei [of the sperm and oocyte] fuse with each other to produce the single, diploid, 2n nucleus of the fertilized *zygote*. This moment of zygote formation may be taken as the beginning or zero time point of embryonic development.[4]

Even those who disagree with this position concede that it is held by the majority of embryologists. For example, referring to this position, Norman Ford says: "Most embryologists would appear to agree," and then quotes several sources, some of which are reproduced above.[5]

What evidence moves biologists almost unanimously to place the beginning of the new human individual's life at fertilization? The biologist seldom belabors the point. Usually he or she simply describes the event and indicates, by the vocabulary used as much as by explicit statement, that fertilization is the

1. Leslie Brainerd Arey, *Developmental Anatomy,* 7th ed. (Philadelphia: Saunders, 1974), 55.

2. Keith L. Moore, *Before We Are Born,* 2d ed. (Philadelphia: Saunders, 1983), 1.

3. Ronan O'Rahilly and Fabiola Mueller, *Developmental Stages in Human Embryos* (Washington, D.C.: Carnegie Institute of Washington, 1987), 9.

4. William J. Larsen, *Human Embryology* (New York: Churchill Livingstone, 1993), 19.

5. Norman Ford, *When Did I Begin?* (New York: Cambridge University Press, 1988), 115.

point where a new individual's life begins. There are, however, at least three considerations that make fertilization the most reasonable point to place the beginning of the new human individual's life.

The first consideration is that the idea that this new organism is the same organism as the one which exists in the womb three weeks later, and then three months later, and so on, is a simple, natural interpretation of the data. To say that the zygote is not the same organism as the one which exists in the womb months later requires one to posit significant changes in addition to what this interpretation requires one to hold. Moreover, one is required to posit these significant changes with no apparent additional agency at work—what transforms the one organism (or more) of one type into another? Or what transforms the cluster of cells into a unified organism?

Secondly, the actual coming to be of a new organism cannot be a gradual process. As Aristotle noted long ago, there are no degrees of being a substance or concrete thing: one either is or is not a horse, one either is or is not an amoeba. Even if the changes which lead to the coming to be of a new organism may be gradual, the transition to actually being one must be instantaneous, and therefore involve a discontinuity. In many cases of substantial change the discontinuity may not be noticeable, but in most cases it is (for example, death, digestion of food, and chemical reactions). Fertilization is a radical discontinuity in a series of events in which it does not seem possible to place the necessary discontinuity anywhere else.

Thirdly, the information which will guide the development of this being is already present within the DNA in the nucleus of the zygote, and the zygote is actively growing. Unlike a dormant acorn, the embryo is actively developing itself. This means that after the fusion of the sperm and the ovum to produce the zygote, the activities of this new organism are organized and directed from within—it grows according to the master plan contained within its genetic code. Of course, not every aspect of its fate is determined—this is not true of anyone. But no organizing information will be added to it from outside after the fusion of sperm and ovum. It is a new center of organization, and it now has within itself the complete capacity to develop itself actively, provided it has suitable nourishment and environment, to the state of a mature human organism.[6]

The eminent French geneticist Jerome Lejeune, after referring to those who say that the human embryo has not yet "humanised," makes the following significant point:

I must say very simply, as a geneticist, I have never heard any specialist in husbandry of animals thinking about the 'cattilisation' of cattle. They know that the embryo of a cow would be a calf. . . . From all the genetic laws that we have tried to summarize, we are entirely convinced that every embryo is, by itself, a human being.[7]

1. Viability, Quickening, and Birth

In popular circles viability is often claimed to be the dividing line between the new human individual and that which is not a human individual. Even the United States Supreme Court, in *Roe v Wade*, used viability as a significant dividing line between that which demands legal protection and that which does

6. The fact that the embryo has a distinctive genetic make-up—in a normal case with the full complement of forty-six chromosomes—does not by itself prove that there now exists a whole, distinct human organism. For in some cases the genetic make-up of this new being is, although in some sense "human," defective to such an extent that it does not have an intrinsic active capacity to develop into a mature human being. These are the cases of hydatidiform moles, or teratomas, and the like. Still, after a normal fertilization process, at this stage—before the first cell division—there exists a distinct organism identical with the organism which will exist there (in the womb) for several months.

7. Quoted in Norman Ford, *When Did I Begin?*, 127. It is taken from the *Official Hansard Report of the Senate Select Committee on the Human Embryo Experimentation Bill 1985*. Cf. Jerome Lejeune, *The Concentration Can: When Does Human Life Begin?* (San Francisco: Ignatius Press, 1992).

not, although in the end the Court made abortions legal even after viability for the sake of the mother's "health," be it physical or mental.[8] It is sometimes argued that if the fetus is not viable, then it is not an independent human being, and only independent human life has intrinsic value or basic rights.

However, viability clearly does not hold up as a criterion for personhood or humanity. As Richard Werner observes, "The difficulty with this criterion is that it rules out as human the man on the heart-lung machine, the woman on the pace-maker, or the old person or baby who is totally dependent on others for their continued existence."[9]

One might try to specify further the notion of viability so that the above groups do qualify as human but fetuses do not. For example, one might say that an entity is viable only if it is not directly dependent on another's body for its continued existence. Still, Werner points out, there would be counterexamples:

In some cases of Siamese twins one member of the pair could be parted from his sibling and go on to live a normal life. However, the second twin is directly dependent on the first twin's body for his existence such that a separation would cause this second twin's death. Now this second twin is certainly not viable in any sense in which an embryo or fetus is not. Yet he is surely a human being.[10]

The idea that viability is a significant dividing line seems based on a confusion of independence with distinctness. The embryo is certainly intimately dependent on his or her mother, but this does not mean that he or she is not distinct. Moreover, there is no reason to think that only those beings not intimately dependent on another being for their continued existence are of intrinsic worth. It is clear that the embryo is a distinct individual and member of the human species before viability.

8. *Roe v Wade,* 410 US 113, 93 S. Ct. 705 (1973) at 156–64, 728–32.

9. Richard Werner, "Abortion: The Ontological and Moral Status of the Unborn," *Social Theory and Practice* 3 (1974): 201–202.

10. Ibid.

For similar reasons, quickening and birth are events which are irrelevant to the question of when a human life begins. Quickening is simply the stage at which the developing organism is large enough for the mother to feel his or her movements in her womb. At birth the baby begins to acquire his or her nourishment and oxygen in a different manner, but can scarcely be viewed as coming to be at that point.

II. Brain Functioning: Brody's Argument

Baruch Brody has presented a position that is close to ours in many respects.[11] An analysis of his position will clarify the positive evidence which exists that an individual human life begins at conception. He agrees that a human being has a right to life from the moment he or she comes to be, and he agrees that the living human being comes to be long before birth. But he places the coming to be of the human being at the point at which he or she has a functioning brain, a point he estimates to be about six weeks into gestation.

Brody argues that the metaphysical position of essentialism is helpful for resolving the controversy concerning when human life begins. According to essentialism, some properties or characteristics are essential and other properties are accidental. A property is essential if a thing cannot lose it without ceasing to be. A property is accidental if it is not essential. Being a tree is an example of an essential property, while having 632 leaves is an accidental property. That is, a tree cannot cease being a tree without ceasing to be, but it can acquire a different number of leaves without ceasing to be. From this perspective, the central question in the abortion controversy is, what is the essential property for membership in the class of living human beings?[12]

11. Baruch Brody, *Abortion and the Sanctity of Human Life: A Philosophical View* (Cambridge: MIT Press, 1975).
12. Ibid., 100–102.

The class of human beings, Brody adds, is a natural kind. He defines a natural kind as a set of objects each of which has a property essentially, with the proviso that nothing else has that property. For example, trees constitute a natural kind, since whatever is a tree is a tree essentially. The class of white objects, on the other hand, is not a natural kind, since being white is not a property which white objects possess essentially (white objects do not go out of existence when they cease to be white).

The question about the humanity of the fetus is, at what point, if any, does the fetus acquire all of the properties necessary for being human? Since humanity is a natural kind, Brody argues, the properties necessary for being human will be essential; that is, they will be properties such that to lose any of them is to go out of existence.

Brody then presents an analysis of death, and he concludes, tentatively, that death is the irreparable cessation of brain function. But if irreparable cessation of brain function marks the going out of existence of the living human being, then brain function is an essential property. Brody also holds that none of the other properties which are acquired after the development of the brain can be plausibly viewed as essential properties. His position is summarized so:

According to what is called the brain-death theory, as long as there has not been an irreparable cessation of brain function the person in question continues to exist, no matter what else has happened to him. If so, it seems to follow that there is only one property—leaving aside those entailed by this one property—had essentially by each human being (and therefore that there is only one property that is essential to humanity), namely, the possession of a brain that has not suffered an irreparable cessation of function.[13]

Before I criticize this position, I would like to note how close it is, nevertheless, to the position I am defending. According

13. Ibid., 107–8.

to Brody's position the vast majority of abortions are homicides. By the time pregnancy is usually suspected the fetus has developed past the stage of beginning to have a functioning brain. His position does, however, imply different moral conclusions regarding RU-486, "morning-after" pills, IUDs, perhaps early fetal experimentation, and so on.

Nevertheless, the difficulties resulting from Brody's view make it untenable. First, the six-week estimate for the beginning of the presence of the brain does not hold up. True, the brain is not complete in its general structure until the sixth week of gestation, but what reason is there for requiring completeness in structure before saying that, basically, the brain is present?

One would require the presence of the human brain for the presence of a living human being for only one of two reasons. First, one might say that the brain is necessary because only then does one have the organic basis for the potentialities characteristic of human beings. But although the gross structure of the brain is present at six weeks into gestation, the brain is not in fact structurally complete until some time after birth, because the connections between the neurons are not developed until some time after birth.[14] And without the synaptic connections, which come *at the earliest* three months after birth, the fetus or infant does not yet have the organic basis for the higher operations of thought. But it is quite implausible to hold that there is no human individual until three or more months after birth. (Recall that we are discussing the argument that the embryo is not *human,* and not the position that it is human but not a person.)

The second reason one might require the presence of the brain is that one argues that not until then is there a single organism. But this is demonstrably false. After the fusion of the sperm with the ovum, the zygote (the result of this fusion)

---

14. See the thorough discussion and references in Michael Tooley, *Abortion and Infanticide* (New York: Oxford University Press, 1983), 357–407.

manifests all the marks of unitary, organic activity: its activities of nourishment and growth are as unified and intelligibly directed as are the activities of any other organism of that size. Long before the appearance of the primitive streak, there is clearly a single "primary organizer," coordinating the various actions of the single, multicellular organism. The primitive streak appears in the third week of gestation.

So, while Brody is correct to insist that what we say about the end of human life should be consistent with what we say about its beginning, he has located the analogy in the wrong place. The reason why irreparable cessation of brain function constitutes death is not because having a brain is at all stages of the human being's life a necessary property, but because in the mature human being the brain is the organ which organizes all of the systems of the human organism. So, when the brain ceases to function (totally and irreparably) in a mature human being, the various tissues and organs cease to form an organism. Now a human being is essentially an organism (a specific type of organism), and so if the tissues and organs cease to constitute an organism, then the human being has ceased to be.

In other words, human beings have several essential properties in the sense that what a human being is can be understood and expressed more or less specifically. Being an organism is an essential property of a human being, albeit a general one. So, if a human being ceases to be an organism, then he or she ceases to be. But also, since being an organism expresses (less specifically) what a human being is, it is impossible for an organism to come to be at one time and, remaining the same organism, become human at a later time. This would make humanity an accidental property of human beings, a position Brody rightly rejects. So, if an organism at one time is the same organism as a human organism at a later time, then the organism at the earlier time is a human organism also, the same human organism as the one which exists at the later time.

In sum, the position that having a developed brain is necessary for a living human being is untenable. On examination, the reasons which first suggest that position lead to different conclusions. The evidence indicates that the same organism exists at conception, at six weeks with a developed brain, and after birth; all of these are stages in the development of the self-same organism. If one grants that human persons are physical organisms—and Brody does grant this—then one should grant that the living human being comes to be at fertilization.

Finally, I wish to comment on Brody's use of the following science-fiction example:

[I]magine that medical technology has reached the stage at which, when brain death occurs, the brain is removed, "liquefied," and "recast" into a new functioning brain. The new brain bears no relation to the old one (it has none of its memory traces, and so on). If the new brain were put back into the old body, would the same human being exist, or a new human being who made use of the body of the old one? I am inclined to suppose the latter.[15]

He then argues that the body of the brain-dead individual is in the relevant respects similar to the fetus:

Both have the potential for developing a functioning brain (we shall call this a weak potential), but neither now has the structure of a functioning brain. We can conclude, it seems to me, that an entity can go out of existence even if it retains a weak potential for having a functioning brain, and analogously, that the fetus is not a human being just because it has this weak potential.[16]

I agree that the new being resulting from inserting the "recast" brain into the body of the former human being would not be the same as that former individual. But Brody is mistaken to think that the situation of the fetus is similar to this case in the relevant respects. First, the two cases would be similar only if in both cases the only continuity were that of the

15. Brody, *Abortion and the Sanctity of Human Life*, 353.
16. Ibid., 114.

body, or rather, of the bodily parts. In the science-fiction example, when the first individual suffers brain death, what survives are the various parts, no longer making up a single organism. Then, the bodily parts of the first individual go into the make-up of the second individual. But the situation of the fetus is not similar in this respect at all. With the fetus the continuity consists in the fact that it is the same *organism,* before the development of the brain and after its development. There is no reason to think that the development of the brain causes the death of that earlier organism, to give way to a distinct organism. Rather, the evidence is that the development of the brain is a stage in the maturation process of the selfsame organism. So, the analogy Brody presents breaks down.

It is worth adding that although Brody refers both to the potential of the bodily parts of the first individual in the science-fiction case and to the potential of the fetus to develop a brain as a "weak potential," the two potentialities are quite different. The potentiality of the bodily parts is a capacity to receive from outside the enlivening and organizing functions of a brain; the potentiality of the fetus is a capacity actively to develop, according to a design intrinsic to it, a brain. To call both of them "weak potential" is to ignore this important difference between them.

III. An Argument Based on Hylomorphism

Another argument for the position that the fetus is not a human being until some time after conception is based on the hylomorphic theory (matter-form theory) of the constitution of human beings. Until recently, the chief proponent of this argument was Joseph Donceel. However, in a recent article in *Theological Studies,* Allan Wolter and Thomas Shannon argue for this position also. They argue that the Thomistic, or scholastic, theory of human beings as composed of matter and soul (or form), that is, *hylomorphism,* is a cogent theory, and that it still supports the conclusion (as Thomas himself thought it did) that the fetus is not a human being from the time of conception. Shannon and Wolter present other arguments in addition to the one based on hylomorphic theory, and we will discuss these in section IV.

According to the hylomorphic theory, all living beings, including humans, are composed of matter and a principle which informs or determines the matter to be one sort of thing, rather than another. This principle is the substantial form, and in living things it is called "soul." The soul of a living thing comes to be when the living thing itself comes to be. However, the soul, like any substantial form, is proportioned to its matter. That is, since the soul is just the organizing principle of living things, it comes to be when the matter becomes organized in a certain way. Therefore, the soul comes to be only when the matter is organized sufficiently (by some agent) to have that form. Donceel expresses these points succinctly: "The main philosophical principles are as follows. The soul is the substantial form of man. A substantial form can exist only in matter capable of receiving it. In the case of man's soul this means: the human soul can exist only in a highly organized body."[17] Later, Donceel adds that at the start of pregnancy a highly organized body is not present: "Yet, at the start there is not at once a highly organized body, a body with sense organs and a brain."[18]

Summarizing his position, Donceel argues, "If form and matter are strictly complementary, as hylomorphism holds, there can be an actual human soul only in a body endowed with the organs required for the spiritual activities of man. We know that the brain, and especially the cortex, are the main organs of those highest sense activities without which no spiritual ac-

17. Joseph Donceel, "Immediate Animation and Delayed Hominization," *Theological Studies* 31 (1970): 79.
18. Ibid., 80.

tivity is possible."[19] Donceel therefore holds that a fetus is not a human being until the cerebral cortex is present.

Essentially the same argument is proposed by Shannon and Wolter in their more recent article. They conclude that the organ necessary for thought is not present until twenty weeks into gestation. They write:

One can speak of a rational nature in a philosophically significant sense only when the biological structures necessary to perform rational actions are present, as opposed to only reflex activities. The biological data suggest that the minimal time of the presence of a rational nature would be around the 20th week, when neural integration of the entire organism has been established. The presence of such a structure does not argue that the fetus is positing rational actions, only that the biological presupposition for such actions is present.[20]

There is an obvious question to ask with regard to this argument. Let us grant, for the sake of argument, that human beings are composed of matter and soul, and that the human soul is the substantial form of the human body, or is related to the body as substantial form is related to matter. And so we also grant, for the sake of argument, that the matter must be proportioned to the form, or soul, that the matter must first be sufficiently organized before it is capable of receiving the human form or soul. Nevertheless, the crucial question is: How much organization is required? Donceel holds that the development of the cerebral cortex is required. Shannon and Wolter hold that the integration of the cerebral cortex with the brain stem, at about twenty weeks, is required.

Although their positions differ, the reason they propose for their positions is the same: human nature's specific difference, and what distinguishes human nature as being on a higher level

19. Ibid., 83.
20. Thomas Shannon and Allan Wolter, "Reflections on the Moral Status of the Pre-Embryo," *Theological Studies* 51 (1990): 620.

than other animals, is reason, and the necessary condition for reasoning is the operation of the cerebral cortex. Henri de Dorlodot, quoted by Donceel, stated the key premise as follows: "Hence a body cannot be informed, i.e., animated, by a life-principle of a particular species, if it does not possess the organization characteristic of the species in question, and in particular, if it has not the organs essential for the species. Again these organs must have the organization proper to the species."[21]

In sum, the argument seems to be:

1. The soul is not present until the organ(s) essential to the species is present.

2. The essential organ(s) is the organ(s) necessary for the operation specific or distinctive of the species (for the operations of things are their fulfillments or actualizations).

3. The operation specific to the human species is reasoning (which we can take to include both thought and will).

4. The principal organ required for reasoning is the brain, more specifically, the cerebral cortex, or the integration of the different parts of the brain.[22]

5. The cerebral cortex, or the integration of the brain's parts, is not present at conception.

6. Therefore, the human soul is not present at conception.

I will first show that the main argument of Donceel and others does not establish its conclusion. Secondly, I will argue that the position itself is mistaken, and that the contrary position, namely, that the conceptus is a human organism from fertil-

21. Henri de Dorlodot, "A Vindication of the Mediate Animation Theory," in *Theology and Evolution,* ed. E. C. Messenger (London: Sands and Co., 1949), 261.

22. This need not be taken to mean that the brain itself performs the operation of thought, only that the brain's operation is a necessary condition of thought, whether the action of thought be performed by means of a bodily organ or not.

ization onwards, is the only reasonable position in the light of the empirical data.

If we grant, with Donceel and others, that matter must always be proportioned to form, and that the human soul can only come to be in an organized body, this very general point is far from the more specific claim that the organs necessary for the operations distinctive of the species must be present before the matter is disposed to receive the soul or form. Anyone holding any type of hylomorphic theory will grant the general point, but no evidence has been offered to support the more specific claim.

Secondly, the argument fails because it is based on too narrow a conception of soul. The proponents of this argument view the soul only in its synchronic function (its effect at a definite time) and ignore its diachronic function (its effect on a sequence spread out in time). They view the soul as the first act of the living thing's present operations. And they argue that if the matter is not organized sufficiently to have the organ necessary for the living thing's specific operations, then the soul of such a living thing is not present. But they ignore the hylomorphic theory's notion of the soul's diachronic function, that is, its function as the immanent design for the series of temporal events which, possessing a certain intelligible relation among them, are recognized as events belonging to a single organism. The intelligibility, the immanent design, here, is that present among a series of events spread out in time, such that the earlier events can only be reasonably interpreted as intrinsically directed to an activity which may take place much later.

On this view the soul is present from the beginning of that intelligible series, not just at its culmination. Often what gives intelligibility to a series of events is some limited number of the series which occurs late in the series. For example, a dog chasing a rabbit: what confers intelligibility on the whole series of events—which includes bounding, zigging and zagging, hopping, and so on—is the event which occurs only very late in the series, namely, the dog's grasping of the rabbit in his teeth. That event confers intelligibility and gives unity to the whole sequence of events which preceded earlier. However, the unifying factor—in this case, the dog's desire to eat the rabbit—must be posited as present throughout the whole sequence of events.[23] In the embryo's case there is ample evidence that its development is intrinsically directed or guided, from fertilization onwards. The most reasonable conclusion, then, is that an organism already exists, that there is an actual unity, a soul, from the moment those events occur which must be seen as fitting into the intelligible pattern of the development of that organism. This moment occurs long before the presence of those organs which make possible the more mature functions of the living thing as a member of its species. Hence, the hylomorphic argument simply ignores one of the key functions of the soul and therefore does not establish its conclusion.

Thirdly, the argument fails because there are several counterexamples to its first premise, that matter must have the organs presupposed by the actions distinctive of the species of the organism before such an organism exists. Reproduction is one of the operations by which living things are distinguished from nonliving. Moreover, reproduction is arguably the highest activity for animals other than human beings. But reproductive organs are not mature and functional for many years in most animals. Some animals function with one set of digestive organs when young and another set when more mature, hence their complete digestive system is not present until long after birth (tadpoles, for example). Again, whatever the distinctive operation of a butterfly is,[24] we can be sure that the organs

23. Cf. Bernard Lonergan, *Insight* (New York: Philosophical Library, 1970), 245–70; Rudolph Gerber, "When Is the Human Soul Infused?" *Laval théologique et philosophique* 22 (1966): 234–47.

24. According to the hylomorphic theory, each species has a distinctive operation.

necessary for that operation are absent at the larva or pupa stage, and yet the larva or the pupa is clearly an individual of the same species as the corresponding butterfly.

Next, I argue against the position itself. It will help to see the difficulties in the position if we take a brief look at Thomas Aquinas's own position (from which this one is derived) and why he held it. Thomas's reason for holding that the fetus was not human just after conception was different from the arguments proposed above. As Benedict Ashley has shown,[25] Thomas's position was more tied to his ignorance of empirical facts concerning conception than the articles by Donceel and Shannon and Wolter might suggest.

Thomas's central position was that the rational soul of a human being must be directly created by God, but that in all other respects the generation of the human being is like the generation of other animals, a process whose principal efficient cause (according to Thomas) is the male parent.[26] This position maintained both the transcendence of matter by the human soul, and an essential role for the male parent (in humans and other animals) as efficient cause. These points were important to Thomas, for in general he emphasized the efficacy and value of secondary causes.

The material cause of the process was, in Thomas's view, the menstrual blood contributed by the mother. The menstrual blood was thought to be nonliving and relatively devoid of organization or differentiation. The efficient cause of the process was the semen. Better, the semen was the instrumental efficient cause, and the male parent was the principal efficient cause. Thomas quite rightly held that there must be an adequate cause

---

25. Benedict Ashley, "A Critique of the Theory of Delayed Hominization," in *An Ethical Evaluation of Fetal Experimentation: An Interdisciplinary Study*, ed. Donald McCarthy and Albert Moraczewski (St. Louis: Pope John XXIII Medical-Moral Research and Education Center, 1976), 113–33.

26. Thomas Aquinas, *Summa theologiae*, Part 1, question 118, articles 1 and 2.

of the process, that this cause must have the power to produce something like itself, that is, a highly complex, organized animal, and that only something as complex and organized as the animal itself could be an adequate cause.

Thomas thought that the semen contained a *vital spirit,* which is the subject or organ for the formative power or force, that is, the power of forming the material contributed by the mother to the point that it is disposed to receive the human soul. The vital spirit was not conceived as a spiritual entity but as a gaseous or ether-like bodily substance.[27] Thus, as Ashley has shown, the reason why Thomas thought that the fetus was not human at conception was that he believed the process required time. That is, he believed that the formative power in the semen had to form nonliving matter to the very high state or organization suitable for the human body. As Ashley expressed it, "Thus Aristotle and Aquinas could only conclude that the formative action of the male parent would have to take place over a considerable period of time before it could temper the menstrual blood to the level of organization required for a human body that would be capable of the highest type of sensitive life."[28]

Another point worth emphasizing is that it was central to Thomas's theory that the semen, or at least the vital spirit of the semen, remain as a distinct agent throughout the whole process until the likeness of the generating parent was induced into the material. There must be an adequate, ongoing cause of the process. The male parent was no longer present. Thomas explicitly rejected the argument that God intervened to produce the souls of animals, including the sensitive soul of the human *conceptus* in the process of human generation.[29] Therefore, he

27. Ibid., article 2.
28. Ashley, "A Critique," 118.
29. Thomas Aquinas, *Summa theologiae,* Part 1, question 118, article 1. On Thomas's position, see also Stephen J. Heaney, "Aquinas and the Presence of the Human Embryo," *The Thomist* 56 (1992): 19–48.

held that the male parent acted by means of the instrumental force in the vital spirit of the semen, and that this force must be present throughout the process. Given his misinformation regarding the empirical biological facts, Thomas's position appears reasonable, and solves the problems presented by what he thought were the data.

But of course we know that Thomas was mistaken on the data. Moreover, his mistakes or ignorance about the data are not peripheral to his view of human generation. First, we now know that the contribution by the mother does not consist in merely providing nonliving menstrual blood. Rather, the ovum is a living, highly organized cell, containing specific information in the genetic structure of the chromosomes in its nucleus, information which will help specify (together with the information provided by the genetic structure in the chromosomes of the male sperm) the development of the new living organism.[30] Thus, the evidence indicates that the ovum is very close to readiness for rapid embryological development. Hence the principal reason why Thomas was moved to say that the process of appropriately disposing the matter should take time is no longer present.

Secondly, we now know that there is nothing in the sperm which remains as a distinct agent in the process of the embryo's development, contrary to what Thomas thought. After fertilization neither the sperm nor the ovum remains. What exists is a distinct organism which then apparently begins a process of self-development oriented to the stage of a mature human adult. This point is important, because it means that, in the light of facts discovered since Thomas's time, contemporary proponents of the theory of delayed animation or hominization posit an event with no apparent empirical cause. The unitary process of the development of the embryo requires an adequate,

30. We also know that spontaneous generation, after which Thomas closely modeled his ideas on animal reproduction, does not occur.

unitary cause. Thomas thought the adequate cause was the male parent, acting by means of the vital spirit from the semen as the instrumental cause. But that will not do, because nothing of the semen remains as a distinct agent. It will not do either to say that the adequate cause of the development of the embryo is the embryo itself, that is, it will not do if one maintains the theory of delayed hominization. For to say that the embryo is the cause is just to say that the embryo is already human and is developing itself to its stage of maturity. Otherwise put, one cannot coherently hold that nonhuman cells simply unite and make themselves human.

Donceel recognizes the problem, and at this point says that the cause we are seeking is God. He writes:

The reader who has been willing to follow me hitherto may wonder how I explain the formation of the new human being. If neither the soul of the father nor the soul of the embryo itself explains embryonic development, where are we to look for the cause of the process? My preference goes to the theory delineated first by Teilhard de Chardin and worked out in detail by Karl Rahner. . . . In this conception the creatures are more than instrumental, less than material, causes for God. . . . Thus embryogeny is explained on the phenomenal level by the countless physiochemical and biological factors, whose activity is investigated with increasing success by the science of embryology; it is explained on the ontological level by the creative power of God. . . .[31]

This move, it seems to me, is a clear instance of a deus ex machina. All of the evidence indicates that the embryo actively develops himself or herself in the process in question, but Donceel sets aside that evidence, and then must posit a special intervention by God to fill the gap left by his denial of empirical evidence.

Shannon and Wolter apparently hold that the required cause is actually the sequence of events. They write:

31. Donceel, "Immediate Animation," 84–85.

[T]he pre-embryonic form as a system is not totally passive, the recipient only of actions from the outside as it were. It has its own activities arising from the released potencies of the novel combination of its constituent materials. Such potencies are released when these elements form a system, e.g. the embryo. This development of new systems gives rise to new activities and possibilities and serves as the foundation or presupposition for other stages of development. Philosophically speaking, we have every reason to believe that the dynamic properties of the organic matter—the elements of the fully formed zygote—owe their existence to their organizational form or the system.[32]

But this sequence, or organizational form or system, is precisely what needs to be accounted for. It is the unity and regularity of this multiplicity of events—the directed growth of the multicellular embryo—that requires a cause.

Finally, as Germain Grisez pointed out, this theory has another, equally serious, inconsistency.[33] Its proponents do not wish to place "hominization" at a point *after* birth, for it is obvious to everyone that the newborn is at least a human organism. And yet were they consistent in their requirement that the "biological presupposition" for mental actions be present before there is a human being with a rational soul, that is where they would have to place it. The brain is certainly present at six weeks and it is functioning even at eight weeks. Also, it is true that the cerebral cortex develops later, present at three months, and connected with the rest of the brain, the brain stem, at about three and a half months. But not until three months after birth, at the earliest, do the nerve cells in the cortex have the kind of connections needed to provide the biological basis for mental or reflective actions.[34] As Grisez puts it, "[T]his beginning of the brain's development (where Donceel placed the bio-

32. Shannon and Wolter, "The Moral Status of the Pre-Embryo," 620.

33. Germain Grisez, "When Do People Begin?" *Proceedings of the American Catholic Philosophical Association* 63 (1990): 27–41.

34. Cf. Tooley, *Abortion and Infanticide*, 357–407.

logical presupposition of thought) is not the bodily basis for intellectual activities but only its precursor."[35]

IV. Twinning and Other Phenomena

Other arguments that the developing embryo is not a human individual from fertilization onwards often refer, in various ways, to the phenomenon of identical twins. Identical twins occur when an early embryo divides and two (or more) distinct organisms are formed. Twinning can occur, apparently, up to the stage that the "primitive streak" appears in the embryo, a sign that its cells have specialized sufficiently so that no longer does each have the potentiality to become an entire embryo (about 14 days). Moreover, up to the stage of the appearance of the primitive streak, it may be possible in some cases for two embryos to combine and form one living embryo.[36] I shall consider four different, though closely related, arguments stemming from such considerations that hold that the embryo is not a human individual after fertilization.

1. A first objection is that before gastrulation (differentiation into layers or folds, at the third week), or before the development of the primitive streak, as long as twinning can still occur, what exists is not yet an individual, but only a mass of cells. Piet Schoonenberg, quoted by Donceel, articulated this argument quite clearly:

One fact especially renders for us a later "hominization" of the embryo more probable: the occurrence of identical twins (triplets, etc.). This fact shows that biologically speaking the fecundated ovum is not yet wholly individual. For, although its hereditary virtualities are set, a cellular division may change it into more than one individual. . . . As long as such a possibility exists, the philosophical definition of individual, which explains it as "undivided

35. Grisez, "When Do People Begin?" 33.
36. The data for such occurrences in humans is sparse.

in itself" (*indivisum in se*), is not yet realized, at least not as strictly as the individuality of the human person demands. If the fecundated ovum can split into two beings which turn out to be two persons, it is difficult to admit that at first it was itself a person, hence fully human.[37]

Shannon and Wolter express the argument in this way:

Because of the possibility of twinning, recombination, and the potency of any cell up to gastrulation to become a complete entity, this particular zygote cannot necessarily be said to be the beginning of a specific, genetically unique individual human being. While the zygote is the beginning of genetically distinct life, it is neither an ontological individual nor necessarily the immediate precursor of one.[38]

Taken literally, this argument is based on a confusion between two different senses of the word "individual" or "undivided." When a person is defined as a certain type of *individual,* the word means *logically* undivided, as opposed to a universal or class, where the property or nature is divided among many.[39] The division of the embryo shows only that he or she is *physically* divisible. Before splitting, the zygote or the two-, four-, or eight-celled embryo is an individual, not a universal. From the fact that A can split into B and C, it simply does not follow, nor does the fact at all suggest, that A was not an individual before the division. It may be that A ceases to be and B and C come to be from the constituents that once went into A (though this is not the most likely situation), or that A is identical with B or C. But the facts simply do not suggest that A did not exist or was not yet individual. All of us are *physically* divisible, but that does nothing to call into question our present individuality in the relevant sense.

37. Donceel, "Immediate Animation," 98–99.
38. Shannon and Wolter, "The Moral Status of the Pre-Embryo," 612.
39. On the notion of individuality in the classical definition of person, see Thomas Aquinas, *Summa theologiae,* Part 1, question 27, article 1.

2. A second objection was presented by Norman Ford. He claims that holding that the very early embryo is an individual human being is incoherent. Proponents of the humanity of the early embryo usually argue that the embryo's active potentiality to develop into a mature human being shows that it already is human. Noting this, Ford argues:

> It would also be more coherent to hold that whilst admitting the zygote is a living individual being, it could not be a human individual on the simple grounds that, given the right conditions, it had the natural active potentiality to develop into an adult. It could, given the right conditions, equally develop into two adult human individuals. It would have to be both one, and more than one, human individual at the same time.[40]

Ford would be right if the "right conditions" in the one case were of the same sort as the "right conditions" in the other case. But they clearly are not. To say that an embryo has the active potentiality to develop into an adult human being, given the right conditions, is to say that given an *appropriate environment,* he or she will develop himself or herself in that direction. However, in order for any given embryo to split and then begin development as two individuals, more than an appropriate environment is needed; some agent must break down the intercellular bonds, weak though they are at this point, connecting the cells of what, to all appearances, is a multicellular organism.

Each somatic cell of our body has the entire genetic code in the DNA in its nucleus. In each cell only a portion of that code is operative, the portion relevant to the specialty of that cell.

---

40. Norman Ford, *When Did I Begin?* 122. Cf.: "In mice it has been shown that each of the cells of the early cluster has essentially the same capability, in isolation, to produce a whole individual as the zygote itself. At least potentially, therefore, the initial cluster is precursor to several later individuals; in fact, in the armadillo the four-celled stage regularly gives rise to four identical offspring" (Clifford Grobstein, *Science and the Unborn* [New York: Basic Books, 1988], 60).

Theoretically, any of our cells could be cloned; that is, a cell could be isolated and something done to the cell to activate it so that it began to replicate using the whole genetic code instead of the restricted part of it relevant to its specialty. One could claim, then, that each cell of our body has the active potentiality, *given the right conditions,* to produce a distinct organism. But of course the right conditions referred to here include much more than just an appropriate environment. Something must be done positively to activate it. Similarly, the right conditions referred to by Ford, for the splitting of a two-, three-, four- or eight-celled embryo into twins, are more than just the appropriate environment.[41]

If a flatworm is cut in two (in the right place) the result is two flatworms. The reason the division does not simply result in death seems to be that the parts of the flatworm have the capacity to de-differentiate. This fact surely does not imply that prior to the division the flatworm is merely an aggregate of cells or tissues. It simply means that the parts of the flatworm have the potential to become a whole flatworm when isolated from the present whole of which they are parts. Likewise, at the early stages of development of the human embryo the cells seem to be as yet relatively unspecialized and therefore can become whole organisms if they are divided and have an appropriate environment after the division. But that fact does not in the least indicate that prior to such an extrinsic division the embryo is an aggregate rather than a single, multicellular organism.[42]

41. The zygote splits into a three-celled stage and then back to the even-numbered totals. The reasons for this are not understood. See Jerome Lejeune, *The Concentration Can,* 38–41.

42. Cf. T. V. Daly, "Identifying the Origin of a Human Life: The Search for a Marker Event for the Origin of Human Life," *St. Vincent's Bioethics Center Newsletter* 5, no. 1 (March 1987): 4–6; T. V. Daly, "Individuals, Syngamy, and the Origin of Human Life: A Reply to Buckle and Dawson," *St. Vincent's Bioethics Center Newsletter* 6, no. 4 (December 1988): 1–7.

3. A third objection, proposed by Ford and others, and repeated by Shannon and Wolter, is very close to the one just examined. It focuses on the totipotency of the cells before gastrulation. ("Totipotency" refers to the ability of a cell, when isolated from other cells, to develop into a whole, mature organism.) Speaking of the blastocyst stage, Ford says, "It would appear that distinct individuation, or the formation of the cells into a distinct ontological individual, could not take place prior to the early blastocyst stage because it is only then that differentiation occurs amongst the cluster of homogeneous cells of the compacted morula, notwithstanding the 'inside-outside' polarity referred to above."[43] It is clear here that the possibility of twinning is not in itself significant, but seems to be only because it shows that at that stage the cells are not yet so specialized that they are no longer totipotent. Ford and Shannon and Wolter think this fact is incompatible with the embryo being a single organism. As Shannon and Wolter express it, "Maximally, one could argue that full individuality is not achieved until the restriction process is completed and cells have lost their totipotency."[44] Clifford Grobstein expresses this same objection, "In normal mammalian development, until implantation is achieved, there is not yet a rudimentary individual or embryo. During the preceding stages, there is only an unorganized aggregate of precursor cells that lies within a cellular peripheral layer. The peripheral layer is busy with preparation for the actual engagement in implantation."[45] But why should the totipotency of the cells be thought to suggest that there is not a single entity? As already mentioned, a flatworm can be divided into two flatworms, and yet is clearly a single organism before that division. This fact shows that the proximate potency of the parts to become a separate whole upon physical

---

43. Ford, *When Did I Begin?* 136.

44. Shannon and Wolter, *"The Moral Status of the Pre-Embryo,"* 620.

45. Clifford Grobstein, *Science and the Unborn* (New York: Basic Books, 1988), 59.

division is in no way incompatible with the present substantial unity of the whole.

Proponents of this argument seem to hold that in a unitary, multicellular organism the parts function as parts of a unitary whole, but that this is not the case with the cells in this system prior to implantation. However, as the flatworm example shows, a totipotency of a part does not show that *prior to the division* the part is not functioning as a part. The proponents of this argument have offered little evidence other than totipotency to indicate that the cells are operating as independent units. Ford does say, at one point, "Prior to implantation, and more obviously when there are no more than eight blastomeres, each cell takes in its own nutrients, thereby showing autonomy in a vitally significant way."[46] But in the sense in which this is true of the blastomeres, it is also true of all other cells, that is, all cells take in their own nutrients.

Moreover, proponents of this argument ignore the decisive evidence of unity and organization in the embryo prior to implantation. First, there is the fact that none of these cells grows, but all of them use their nutrients to supply the energy needs for cell division. Second, the fact that they are contained within the zona pellucida does not just "give the appearance of unity," as Ford claims, but is itself an important piece of evidence for substantial unity.[47]

46. Ford, *When Did I Begin?* 137.

47. Anthony Fisher writes: "Ford asserts, again as a matter of biological fact, that despite their close contact and the appearance of a single organism or unity, the several cells of an embryo are really distinct organisms: the membranes of these cells 'merely touch', and in early stages are held 'loosely together' in 'simple contact' by gluey junctions and the 'cage' of the protective zona pellucida [125, 137–139, 146]. Once more, little evidence is offered for this interpretation, which runs quite contrary to the understanding of most biologists, or of any ordinary view of photographs of a multicellular embryo with the cells firmly pressed against each other, restricting each other's shape and position" (Fisher, " 'When Did I Begin?' Revisited," *Linacre Quarterly* 58 (1991): 60).

Again, the evidence clearly indicates that the zona pellucida, chorion and placental tissues are not "extra-embryonic" tissues, as Ford claims. Rather, as Anthony Fisher argues, these tissues seem to be "formed by the embryo, usually with its genetic constitution, and for its sole benefit and use, and are indeed its organs: they are clearly not the mother's organs, nor a tumor, nor some alien third organism living symbiotically with mother and embryo."[48] Such activities—formation of organs for the benefit of the whole—constitute the defining trait of organisms.

Further, as indicated, the initial cell divisions result in totipotential cells. Genetic restriction of the cells begins after day five, at the blastocyst stage. But the evidence also shows that the time that this begins to occur is determined from within, by a "clock mechanism" intrinsic to the developing embryo. As explained in a 1982 study on embryology edited by C. R. Austin and R. V. Short:

There appears to be an inbuilt 'clock' in the timing of blastocyst differentiation. When cleavage is delayed or arrested, or when the number of cells in an embryo is reduced artificially, the secretion of blastocoelic fluid occurs at approximately the same time as in intact blastocysts. The 'clock' is not necessarily related to chronological age, and it could be provided by the number of nuclear or cytoplasmic divisions in the embryo. The 'clock' appears to be set and, if development is delayed, the embryo makes up for the delay later.[49]

The operation of this "clock mechanism" is an action which seems directed to the growth and maintenance of the whole, multicellular organism, and therefore is strong evidence for its substantial unity. These facts show not just a general goal-directedness, but an intrinsic goal-directedness.

48. Ibid.
49. Anne McLaren, "The Embryo," in *Reproduction in Mammals,* bk. 2, *Embryonic and Fetal Development,* ed. C. R. Austin and R. V. Short, 2d ed. (Cambridge: Cambridge University Press, 1982), 682–83.

Finally, most important of all, there is considerable evidence that the cells are in fact functioning in distinct ways even from the two-cell stage. Compaction occurs very early, at the eight-cell stage, that is, on the third day. A standard, contemporary embryology text describes the event as follows:

Starting at the eight-cell stage of development, the originally round and loosely adherent blastomeres begin to flatten, developing an inside-outside polarity that maximizes cell-to-cell contact among the blastomeres at the center of the mass. As differential adhesion develops, the outer surfaces of the cells become convex and their inner surfaces become concave. This reorganization, called *compaction,* involves the activity of cytoskeletal elements in the blastomeres.[50]

But, as Benedict Ashley points out, it is unlikely that this event could occur without some prior genetic decoding and communication between the cells, since the cell divisions continue to take place in the orderly, species-specific sequence or pattern.[51]

Even before compaction, the positional differences between the cells is important, the top from the bottom, the right from the left, even though this differentiation is reversible.[52] This point is crucial, for it shows that the cells are functioning differently within the multicellular embryo even while they are still totipotent (again, "totipotency" refers to what they would do if isolated from the whole). As Ashley and Moraczewski point out in a recent article, discussing Ford's position:

The most telling argument of all against Ford is that if this hypothesis were correct, then since the blastomeres are totipotent and

---

50. Larsen, *Human Embryology,* 19. Cf.: "Less obvious, but demonstrable now by electron microscopy, is that the tightly connected cells on the outside have taken on a different internal structure—they have in fact begun their 'differentiation' . . ." (C. R. Austin, *Human Embryos: The Debate on Assisted Reproduction* [Oxford: Oxford University Press, 1989], 10–11, as cited in Ashley, "Delayed Hominization," 177–78).

51. Ashley, "Delayed Hominization," 167–68.

52. Ibid.

(according to that hypothesis) not in communication with each other within the zona pellucida, they should each develop into a mature organism. But in fact they do so only if they are *separated* from the others. This shows that at least some interaction is taking place between them within the zona pellucida which restrains them from individually developing as *whole* organisms and normally directs them collectively to remain *parts* of a single organism continuous with the zygote.[53]

Thus, the evidence indicates that internal differentiation, and internal organization of the activities of the cells, is present from the two-cell stage.

4. Finally, a fourth objection, proposed by Shannon and Wolter and others, claims that the zygote does not have full informational determination, but receives it only later from maternal molecules. Citing an essay by C. A. Bedate and R. C. Cefalo in the *Journal of Medicine and Philosophy*,[54] they write, "Note also that the zygote does not possess sufficient genetic information within its chromosomes to develop into an embryo that will be the precursor of an individual member of the human species."[55] Bedate and Cefalo argued that prior to gastrulation the cell divisions are guided by the RNA from the maternal mitochondria. Thus, Bedate and Cefalo postulate a reception of information from the maternal organism: "Some type of interaction between molecules of the zygote and extra-zygote molecules must occur, because a stage develops at which the blastocyst is established in the uterus with absolute physiological dependence on the mother."[56]

53. Benedict Ashley and Albert Moraczewski, "Is the Biological Subject of Human Rights Present from Conception?" in *The Fetal Tissue Issue: Medical and Ethical Aspects,* ed. Peter Cataldo and Albert Moraczewski (Braintree, Mass.: Pope John Center, 1994), 49.

54. C. A. Bedate and R. C. Cefalo, "The Zygote: To Be or Not to Be a Person," *Journal of Medicine and Philosophy* 14 (1989): 641–45.

55. Shannon and Wolter, "The Moral Status of the Pre-Embryo," 608.

56. Bedate and Cefalo, "The Zygote," 643.

A major argument for this position is their belief that a biologically complete zygote could still give rise to a hydatidiform mole. Thus Bedate and Cefalo argue, "However, the zygote can give rise to a biological entity that is not a person, e.g., a hydatidiform mole. Therefore, an individual zygote, even when biologically perfect, does not possess in itself all the necessary, and surely not sufficient, information to become a human person."[57] Bedate and Cefalo, and Shannon and Wolter following them, argue therefore that the development of the zygote depends on "the actualization of pieces of information that originate *de novo* during the embryonic process, and exogenous information independent of the control of the zygote."[58]

However, one of the claims made by Bedate and Cefalo has been clearly refuted. Antoine Suarez has shown that hydatidiform moles arise from defects in the fertilization process. Complete hydatidiform moles arise from the formation of androgenetic eggs, eggs with two paternal nuclei.[59] This falsifies the claim of Bedate and Cefalo, repeated by others, that a biologically complete zygote might still give rise to a hydatidiform mole. A normal zygote does not subsequently become a hydatidiform mole. Rather, such a growth is simply the result of an incomplete fertilization.[60]

57. Ibid., 644.

58. Shannon and Wolter, "The Moral Status of the Pre-Embryo," 608. See also Thomas Bole, "Metaphysical Accounts of the Zygote as a Person," *Journal of Medicine and Philosophy* 14 (1989): 647–53.

59. Antoine Suarez, "Hydatidiform Moles and Teratomas Confirm the Human Identity of the Preimplantation Embryo," *Journal of Medicine and Philosophy* 15 (1990): 627–35. According to Suarez, the distinction between a "complete" and a "partial" hydatidiform mole is this: The first results from a sperm fertilizing an ovum in which the female pronucleus is absent, the second from two or more sperms fertilizing an apparently normal ovum.

60. "Eggs which develop into CHM (complete hydatidiform moles) carry a gross chromosomal aberration and are from the point of view of the developing capacity equivalent to sperms, oocytes, or isolated epithelial cells, i.e., on principle they cannot develop to term; the same is true of the majority

Moreover, Suarez argues that empirical evidence shows that the embryo receives no new organizing information from the mother. Suarez argues that a comparison of hydatidiform moles with teratomas indicates that maternal molecules do not have an informational influence on the embryo.[61] Suarez concludes: "[T]he postimplantation embryo does not receive any message or information from the mother able to control the mechanisms of development. The biological identity of the human embryo is not determined by the influence of the maternal environment, but depends basically on the information capacity of the embryo itself."[62] It does not appear that any informational factors

---

of eggs which are spontaneously aborted; it is well known today that such eggs cannot develop to term because of gross chromosomal or structural anomalies" (Ibid., 629–30).

61. Suarez points out that if an androgenetic egg is placed within an embryo and thus receives information from both the paternal and maternal genomes, its cells differentiate like the cells of a normal embryo. And, except for the growth being unorganized, the cellular differentiation occurring in teratomas is the same as that which occurs in postimplantation embryos. "If the physiologic interaction with the mother were the cause of the cellular differentiation of the postimplantation embryo, the same interaction should cause androgenetic eggs to develop into teratomas [whose cellular differentiation is of the same type] rather than into CHM [hydatidiform moles of the complete type, which is in fact the result of their growth].

"The fact that malignant teratocarcinomic cells behave like early embryonic cells if they are put into an embryo, is a striking demonstration that the positional information only originates if the domain governed by embryonic information remains well separated from the domain governed by maternal information" (Ibid., 630).

62. Ibid. Bole argues, however, that it is possible for "partial" hydatidiform moles, in some cases, to develop from biologically perfect zygotes; see Bole, "Metaphysical Accounts," 647–53. Bole concludes that, "because the difference between a child and such a mole must be effected by something in addition to the internal organizational principle of the zygote, the facts support Bedate and Cefalo" (653). This argument, however, is fallacious. If Bole is right in the facts he cites, they suggest that some information in addition to what is internal to the zygote must be posited to account for the difference between the partial hydatidiform mole and the relatively mature human embryo. But it does not follow that additional informational factors

are derived from the maternal molecules, contrary to what Bedate and Cefalo and others following them have claimed.

However, more importantly, even if it were true that some information is received from maternal molecules, this would not show that the preimplantation embryo was not a complete human individual. There is no reason to expect that *all* of the future features of the developing organism should be already determined by its internal genetic make-up. Environmental conditions, which could include maternal molecules within the uterus, can determine many of the future characteristics of the developing organism. Indeed, throughout his or her life, many of this organism's important characteristics will arise from interaction between his or her own internal power and the environment. If informational factors are received from maternal molecules, still, how this information fits within the overall development of this organism is determined from within by the organism's own directed growth. Thus, if any information is received from maternal molecules, it does not determine the primary organization and direction of the multitude of cell differentiations and acquisitions and uses of nutrition occurring in this organic system. That primary organization comes from within the embryo itself.[63]

---

are needed for the development of a more mature human. It is entirely consistent with the cited fact that, when a partial hydatidiform mole results, something external to the biologically complete zygote damages, or rather destroys, the basic capacity intrinsic to that zygote. However, no additional factor is needed to change the informational capacity of the zygote in those cases that do result in a more developed human embryo. Moreover, the rarity of cases of partial hydatidiform moles is evidence for this last hypothesis. What has an internal cause should happen with relative frequency and regularity.

63. On this point, see Albert Moraczewski, "Personhood: Entry and Exit," in *The Twenty-Fifth Anniversary of Vatican II: A Look Back and a Look Ahead,* Proceedings of the Ninth Bishops' Workshop, Dallas, Tex., ed. Russell E. Smith (Braintree, Mass.: Pope John Center, 1990), 94–101; and Benedict Ashley, "Delayed Hominization: Catholic Theological Perspective," in *The Interaction of Catholic Bioethics and Secular Society,* Proceedings of the Elev-

Having shown that arguments for the hypothesis proposed by Ford and others fail, I now argue that the hypothesis itself has insuperable difficulties. In effect the proposal is that, first, the unitary, single-celled zygote is formed by the fusion of the sperm and ovum, then it splits into several independent organisms, only to be reunited some three weeks later to form a multicellular organism. No explanation is provided for what guides this process. Nothing seems to happen at the point of the appearance of the primitive streak (the point which Ford proposes as the initiation of the individual) that might account for the sudden appearance of unity among the previously manifold cells. Only at fertilization, with the fusion of sperm and ovum, is there any event which could be construed as imposing unity on what was previously manifold. In effect, the hypothesis amounts to saying that fertilization is not completed until the primitive streak stage. But there is a wealth of evidence to go against this supposition. This evidence indicates that prior to the primitive streak stage there is already a regularly occurring, predictable, orderly sequence of events of division, differentiation, and growth, beginning with the one-celled organism and leading to an organism with a clear precursor of a brain. I conclude that the more reasonable position is the one taken by the majority of embryologists, that the beginning of the life of the new individual human occurs at the fusion of sperm and ovum.

v. Incomplete Fertilizations and "Wastage"

Two objections to this position which are often raised in this context remain to be considered. Sometimes abnormal fertilization results in a hydatidiform mole, without the potentiality to develop into a more mature, whole human being. This mass

---

enth Bishops' Workshop, Dallas, Tex., ed. Russell E. Smith (Braintree, Mass.: Pope John Center, 1992), 163–79.

of tissue is genetically distinct from the mother, is human, but is clearly not a whole human being. One might object that this occurrence shows that a human person does not begin at conception, but at some later moment in time.

The fact that the fertilization process can fail, however, does not show that even when it succeeds a new human being has not yet been formed. A hydatidiform mole does not have, and never did have, the epigenetic primordia of a human body with the capacities of a mature human (at least some intellectual act). Rather, the hydatidiform mole has *within itself* something which predetermines it to develop only into unorganized tissues. Thus, in a successful fertilization the new individual is a whole, although immature, human being. In an unsuccessful fertilization process resulting in a hydatidiform mole, the resulting individual is not a whole human being. The conceptual situation is like that of a man's heart which is kept beating after he has died or a number of human cells in a petri dish.[64]

Finally, theological considerations have sometimes been proposed for setting a cutoff point later than fertilization. A certain percentage of fertilized ova fail to implant, and often the woman is not even aware a fertilization has occurred. When this percentage is added to the percentage that miscarry later in pregnancy for various reasons, and one holds that the beginning of an individual's life is at fertilization, the percentage of humans who never reach birth may seem quite high. It is argued, then, that God would not allow such "wastage." Shannon and Wolter say that only 45 percent of fertilized eggs come to term, the other 55 percent miscarrying for various reasons. They argue then, "Such vast embryonic loss intuitively argues against the creation of a principle of immaterial individuality at conception. What meaning is there in the creation of such a principle when there is such a high probability that this entity will not develop to the embryo stage, much less come to

64. Grisez, "When Do People Begin?" 39.

term?"[65] In fact, in a footnote they claim, "To ascribe such bungling of the conceptual process to an all-wise creator would seem almost sacrilegious."[66]

There are two points to make in reply to such a bold claim. First, the percentages mentioned by proponents of this argument are disputable. For one thing, as I argued above, in many cases the fertilization process is in effect incomplete, so that what is growing is not a complete human being. Many of the products of fertilization which fail to implant are no doubt the results of incomplete fertilizations and so are not human persons.[67]

Secondly, arguments from what God would or would not do are, unless based on a revelation of God's own judgment of the matter, too ambitious for our limited intelligences. It is ambitious, to say the least, to argue against an alleged fact on the grounds that God could have no possible use for it. If the attribution of a "wastage" of 55 percent is "almost sacrilegious," what are we to say of the fact that up until quite recently—in other words, for centuries—the infant mortality rate has been higher than that? Given that there is an all-wise God, such an infant mortality rate shows that what Shannon and Wolter call a high degree of "wastage" is not incompatible with divine wisdom.

65. Shannon and Wolter, "The Moral Status of the Pre-Embryo," 619.
66. Ibid., 618.
67. On this point see Ashley and Moraczewski, "Is the Biological Subject of Human Rights Present from Conception?" 47.

4

Is Abortion Justified as Nonintentional Killing?

In this chapter I examine the argument that abortions, or many abortions, are morally right because they are not intentional killing, or, as it is often described, indirect, as opposed to direct, killing. As I shall explain, this is an accurate way of describing the positions of, for example, Judith Jarvis Thomson and Martha Brandt Bolton. Along the way I shall also reply to the argument that killing the fetus is justified because the fetus is an aggressor, a denial that abortion is the intentional killing of an *innocent* person. The main proponent of the position I examine in this chapter has been Judith Thomson, in her famous article, "Defense of Abortion," although others have presented essentially the same position.[1] I will focus chiefly on Thomson's presentation but will also refer to others.

1. Judith Jarvis Thomson, "A Defense of Abortion," in *The Problem of Abortion,* ed. Joel Feinberg, 2d ed. (Belmont, Cal.: Wadsworth, 1984), 173–

1. Thomson's Arguments

Thomson grants for the sake of argument that a fetus is a person from conception on, but she argues that even if this premise of opponents of abortion is granted, it does not follow that abortion is always immoral. She expresses the argument she wishes to respond to as follows:

> Every person has a right to life. So the fetus has a right to life. No doubt the mother has a right to decide what shall happen in and to her body; everyone would grant that. But surely a person's right to life is stronger and more stringent than the mother's right to decide what happens in and to her body, and so outweighs it. So the fetus may not be killed; an abortion may not be performed.[2]

Her reply to this position is to grant that the fetus has a right to life (at least for the sake of argument) but to deny that this right entails that the fetus has the right to everything she needs to sustain her life, in particular to the use of the woman's body. Thomson holds that the mother does not have a right to secure the death of the fetus. Her position thus differs from those we examine in other chapters. She argues, rather, that the mother is not obligated to provide life support for the child in the form of the use of her body.[3] The woman may, therefore, expel the fetus from her womb, if carrying the fetus to term would involve a great sacrifice on her part.

To explain her position further, she makes the following now famous comparison:

---

87. See also, e.g., Martha Brandt Bolton, "Responsible Women and Abortion Decisions," in *Having Children: Philosophical and Legal Reflections on Parenthood,* ed. Onora O'Neill and William Ruddick (New York: Oxford University Press, 1979); and F. M. Kamm, *Creation and Abortion: A Study in Moral and Legal Philosophy* (New York: Oxford University Press, 1992).

2. Thomson, "A Defense," 174.

3. Ibid., 187.

But now let me ask you to imagine this. You wake up in the morning and find yourself back to back in bed with an unconscious violinist. A famous unconscious violinist. He has been found to have a fatal kidney ailment, and the Society of Music Lovers has canvassed all the available medical records and found that you alone have the right blood type to help. They therefore kidnapped you, and last night the violinist's circulatory system was plugged into yours, so that your kidneys can be used to extract poisons from his blood as well as your own. The director of the hospital now tells you, "Look, we're sorry the Society of Music Lovers did this to you—we would never have permitted it if we had known. But, still, they did it, and the violinist now is plugged into you. To unplug you would be to kill him. But never mind, it's only for nine months. By then he will have recovered from his ailment, and can safely be unplugged from you." Is it morally incumbent on you to accede to this situation?[4]

Thomson argues that it is not. And she argues that pregnancy is analogous in the relevant respects to being hooked up to the famous violinist. And so, she concludes, just as it would be morally permissible to detach oneself from the violinist, so it is morally permissible, in many abortion cases, for the woman to remove the fetus from her body.

Although in her original article Thomson equated both the violinist case and permissible abortions with "direct killing," she later emended this judgment.[5] As mentioned earlier, Thomson explicitly distinguishes between securing the death of the fetus, which she says is not morally permissible, and removing the fetus from the mother's body, an action she says is morally permissible if carrying the child involves great sacrifice for the mother. Thus, her argument can be accurately expressed as follows: There is a distinction between intentional killing (secur-

4. Ibid., 174–75.

5. Judith Jarvis Thomson, "Rights and Deaths," in *Rights, Restitution, and Risk,* ed. William Parent (Cambridge: Harvard University Press, 1986), 23–24.

ing someone's death) and bringing about death as a side effect. Many abortions are cases of bringing about death as a side effect, and instances of choosing not to make a great sacrifice, rather than refusing to make a small one. Thus, many abortions are morally right.

Thomson considers the argument that the woman has a responsibility to the child because she voluntarily performed an action, sexual intercourse, which could result in a child. Thomson replies that, first, this position would then have to admit that abortion in the case of pregnancies resulting from rape are permissible. Secondly, a woman may have tried to avoid a pregnancy from her sexual intercourse by using contraception, and so having sexual intercourse by itself does not mean one has voluntarily assumed responsibility for the fetus. Ultimately, her position is that doing what could result in a child being dependent on you is not the same as voluntarily assuming responsibility for a child, and only the latter gives the child a right to your care and nurturing.

This also is her answer to the objection that the woman has a special responsibility to the child in virtue of being her mother. She denies that a biological relationship by itself can establish such a special responsibility.

Surely we do not have any such "special responsibility" for a person unless we have assumed it, explicitly or implicitly. If a set of parents do not try to prevent pregnancy, do not obtain an abortion, but rather take it home with them, then they have assumed responsibility for it, they have given it rights, and they cannot *now* withdraw support from it at the cost of its life because they now find it difficult to go on providing for it.[6]

Thomson also holds that if the burden of a pregnancy is *not* a large sacrifice, then, although it would not be unjust to have an abortion, it would be indecent, that is, immoral, and perhaps as gravely immoral as an injustice would be. If the violinist

6. Ibid., 186.

only needed to be plugged into you for one hour, then, she says, you should allow it. And in the same way: "It would be indecent in the woman to request an abortion, and indecent in a doctor to perform it, if she is in her seventh month, and wants the abortion just to avoid the nuisance of postponing a trip abroad."[7] We are required, as she puts it, to be "Minimally Decent Samaritans," though we are not required to be Good Samaritans. In many cases of pregnancy the woman would be making a large sacrifice for the child, would be acting as a Good Samaritan, if she continued the pregnancy, and that is not morally required of her. Therefore, she concludes, many abortions are morally justified.

II. Thomson's Argument and Child Abandonment

A first indication that Thomson's analysis is flawed is the inadequacy of the reason she gives, in passing, against child abandonment. She says that after you take the child home the child has a right to be cared for because you have voluntarily assumed responsibility to provide him or her with care; the parents have given the child a right to that care. But suppose that the only reason a woman did not get an abortion was that she could not afford one. She and her husband take the child home only because they had no alternative. Moreover, they live in a society where people are not in line to adopt a baby. And so the baby is several days old before anything can be done. If they abandon the baby and then the baby is found, he or she will simply be returned to them. Would it not, according to the analysis Thomson has given, be permissible for these parents to abandon the child in some isolated place—not to secure the child's death, but to detach the child from them, although this would most likely result in the child's death?

Someone might accept this application of Thomson's argu-

7. Ibid., 187.

ment, but I think we can see that abandoning a child in such a situation would be morally wrong. I think we recognize the truth that even reluctant parents have responsibilities to their children. When we read or see on the news that people have left their newborn child in a garbage dumpster we react with horror or disgust. I believe Thomson's argument would lead to condoning such acts, but I also believe that such acts are clearly immoral. Thomson's position has implications which should at least cause one to pause and reconsider.

III. Intentional Killing and Causing Death as a Side Effect

The heart of Thomson's argument concerns the distinction between intentional killing and causing death as a side effect. In her original article she claimed that unhooking the violinist would be direct killing, that is, intentional killing, but that since it would clearly be permissible to unplug the violinist, some cases of direct killing (intentional killing) are permissible. However, in her reply to John Finnis she concedes that unhooking the violinist would not be direct killing.[8] Indeed, Thomson's central claim is that in many instances abortion is a case of not providing life support, rather than a case of intentional killing. Whether she is comfortable with the distinction or not, her argument rests on the distinction between intentional killing and causing death as a side effect, or at least between intentional killing and letting die. She makes this distinction when she says that she is arguing for the permissibility of some abortions, and not for the right to secure the death of the unborn child, and when she argues that one may unplug the violinist, but not, if he miraculously survives, slit his throat.[9] She is careful to maintain such a distinction whenever

8. Thomson, "Rights and Deaths," 23–24.
9. Thomson, "A Defense," 187.

she summarizes her position. For example: "I am arguing only that having a right to life does not guarantee having either a right to be given the use of or a right to be allowed continued use of another person's body—even if one needs it for life itself."[10]

I will argue that Thomson is correct to say that not every abortion is intentional killing, but I will also argue that most abortions are intentional killing. Secondly, I will argue that even if some abortions are not intentional killing, they are not morally justified, except perhaps in some cases to save the mother's life. To begin, though, we need first to clarify the distinction between intentional killing and causing death as a side effect, and we can do this using Thomson's example of the violinist plugged into one's kidneys. The difference is that between what one wills as an end or as a means (what one intends) and what one foresees that one will cause as a side effect (sometimes described as what one "indirectly wills"). What one wills or intends is, first, what one sees as desirable in itself, an end, and, secondly, what one sees as bringing about what one desires for its own sake, the means. One wills an end; one chooses an action to bring about that end; and then one performs the behavior which puts into effect, or executes, one's choice. The physical behavior causes more than what one wills as an end or as a means. What is caused by one's behavior but not willed as an end or as a means is a side effect of one's action. One has some responsibility for a foreseen side effect, for one could have acted differently, but one's will is not related to a side effect in the same way that it is related to what one intends.[11]

In the example of the violinist, if you unplug him from your kidneys then, presumably, what you will as an end is to go about your other business, and what you choose as a means is

10. Ibid., 180.

11. On this point see Germain Grisez and Joseph Boyle, *Life and Death with Liberty and Justice* (Notre Dame: University of Notre Dame Press, 1979), 381–92.

detaching him from your body. His death does not contribute to your end at all, and so it is a side effect of what you intend, rather than being itself intended.

On the other hand, if someone threatens you with death unless you torture someone to death (an example mentioned by Thomson) and you accede to his demand, then you cannot claim that the victim's death is only a side effect. In that case, the victim's death is necessary to bring about your end, and is chosen and willed as a means toward your end of appeasing the blackmailer.

I will argue in chapter 5 that it is never morally right to intend the death or killing of an innocent human being, but that in some cases it is morally right to cause death as a side effect. I think Thomson is right that there are some cases of abortion in which the death (or killing) of the child is not willed or intended, but is a side effect of what is willed or intended. Suppose the woman dislikes the prospect of bodily changes due to pregnancy, or that she is frightened by the prospect of the discomfort and pain of childbirth. Or suppose, what is more serious than these, that she has a heart condition and the pregnancy would put a strain on her heart. In each of these cases what the woman wills to avoid by having the abortion is precisely the condition of pregnancy. That is her end. The means by which this end is attained is the removal of the child from the womb. If the child is too young, then the child will die when removed from the womb. But the death, or killing, of the child is a side effect. If what the woman wills precisely is her not-being-pregnant, then the child's death is not necessary to bring about this end, but is a side effect of the behaviors performed to carry out the choice.[12] This is not to say that abortion in these cases is morally justified, or even that it is less

12. If A is not a necessary condition for B, then that is a sign that A is not willed as a means toward B. However, this proposition cannot be transposed. That is, it is not true that if A is a necessary condition of B, then A is a means toward B.

gravely wrong than many cases of intentional killing. It is only to say that Thomson is right that some abortions are not intentional killing.

Some hold that every choice of abortion must be a direct killing, that is, an intentional killing. Their answer to Thomson is different from mine; they deny her major premise, whereas I deny that her conclusion follows from her major premise. That is, I argue that, even though some cases of abortion may not be intentional killing, they are morally wrong for a different reason. One might argue that every abortion must be intentional killing because one must intend everything that one knows to be physically included in the physical act one chooses to bring about. But in abortion one chooses the removal of the baby, knowing that this physically includes the baby's being killed. One cannot, then, according to this argument, choose the removal of the baby without choosing the killing of the baby.[13]

This argument, however, does not seem correct. It does not seem true that one must intend whatever one knows to be physically identical with what one does intend as the end (something desirable in itself) or as bringing about (or helping to bring about) the end (the means). In other words, what one intends, or directly wills, is just the end and that part of reality that one is caused to will insofar as one thinks it will bring about, or help bring about, the end. One may foresee that the physical reality one causes, or the behavior one performs, to bring about what one has chosen may physically include more than one wills either as an end or as a means. Those realities are side effects of what one intends or directly wills. This point follows from the fact that intention is not a physical relation, but is an act specified by what one understands; only if it were a physical

13. See, e.g., Kevin Flannery, "What is Included in a Means to an End," *Gregorianum* 74 (1993): 499–513; and Robert Barry, "Thomson and Abortion," in *Abortion: A New Generation of Catholic Responses,* ed. Stephen J. Heaney (Braintree, Mass.: Pope John Center, 1992), 163–76.

relation would it follow that if someone, S, intends x, and x is known to be physically identical with y, then S must intend y.

Consider this example: Jones's clothes are on fire; I grab a bucket of water, which I know also has marbles in it, to throw onto Jones. My will is clearly related differently to the event, *my throwing marbles on Jones,* than to the event, *my throwing water on Jones.* This is clear even though, physically, my throwing the water on him is identical with my throwing the marbles on him. I may try to throw the water-with-marbles onto him in such a way as to throw as few marbles as possible, knowing it is impossible to throw no marbles at him. Here my physically throwing water at Jones is physically identical with my physically throwing marbles at Jones, but I only intend the former and not the latter. This point is clear, since I could not try to prevent the throwing of the marbles onto him if I were simultaneously directly willing to do so.[14]

14. A similar example: if a physical defect caused me to stutter, I might intend to speak, foresee that the physical act of speaking will include stuttering, and try to prevent my stuttering as much as possible. Again, although the speaking and the stuttering are physically identical, I would intend only the former and not the latter. (Joseph Boyle and Thomas Sullivan use this example to show that there must be a distinction between what is intended and foreseen side effects; see Boyle and Sullivan, "The Diffusiveness of the Intention Principle: A Counter-Example," *Philosophical Studies* 31 [1977]: 357–60.)

According to the traditional position on self-defense, one may use force to stop the attack, even if one foresees that this force will also kill the attacker (see Thomas Aquinas, *Summa theologiae,* Part II-II, question 64, article 7). This position presupposes that a state of affairs, such as the attacker's being killed, may be outside the intention of the agent, even though it is physically identical, or equally physically immediate, with the attacker's being stopped, which is the agent's means and is intended. The important point is that it is not the death which stops the attack, even though his being killed and his being stopped may be simultaneous. Similarly, in some cases of abortion it might be that it is not the death of the unborn baby which brings about the end desired by those choosing the abortion, but the death is a side effect. That, of course, as I explain in the text, does not mean that such acts are morally justified.

Setting aside cases where those making the choice are ignorant of what is being destroyed in abortion, it does seem that abortions in which the death of the child is only a side effect are in the minority. Only rarely is it simply avoiding the condition of pregnancy that is desired (willed). Except in rare cases, what the parties involved desire is the absence of responsibility for a new child. Now, there are two ways of bringing it about that one is not responsible for a child. One is to arrange for someone else to fulfill those responsibilities, that is, to put the child up for adoption. The other is to bring it about that there is no child. So, if the end is not-being-responsible for a child, and adoption is not chosen, then the abortion is a way of bringing it about that there is no child. The death of the child is the means chosen to end responsibility. So, most cases of abortion are intentional killing.[15]

Even in cases where what seems uppermost in the minds of those choosing abortion is the cessation of the condition of pregnancy, this motive may often be mixed with revenge toward the baby as the cause of the undesired condition, or, in rape cases for example, the baby may be hated through association with the child's father. So, again, most abortions (setting aside cases of ignorance) involve willing the child's death.

Moreover, at least most of the cases of abortions which are not intentional killing are still objectively immoral. While it is not always morally wrong to cause death as a side effect, it is not always morally right, either. The question is, what criteria are there for determining when causing death as a side effect is right and when it is not? And, how do those criteria apply to the abortion case?

There are two types of abortions which are not intentional killing, and where the mother's life is not significantly in dan-

15. In most abortions, if by some miracle the baby did survive and the attendants at the clinic brought the baby into the mother, all of those involved in choosing the abortion would no doubt protest that the abortion clinic had not done its job.

ger. In one type, the man and the woman voluntarily perform an action which they realize could result in the procreation of a child. I will argue that in these cases causing the child's death as a side effect is unjust because (a) they have a specific duty to the child since they placed him or her in that dependence relationship, and (b) the harm caused to the child is immensely worse than the harm that the woman (and the others involved) is avoiding by having the abortion. In the second type of case, abortion is performed during a pregnancy due to rape or incest. In this case, (a) does not apply. Still, because of (b) and other reasons which I will discuss in the next section, abortion is not morally right in this type of case, either. Finally, if the mother's life is significantly in danger, then (b) does not apply, and if the choice to save the mother rather than the child is fair (for example, if both cannot be saved), then I have no philosophical argument against abortion in that case, since it seems that it would be causing the child's death as a side effect and with a grave reason to do so.[16] In this section I will discuss abortions which are not intentional killing, where the mother's life is not significantly in danger, and where the sexual intercourse which caused the child is voluntary. In the next section abortion in pregnancies due to rape will be discussed.

Some analogies will help clarify this question. Suppose a man's wife is diagnosed as having a bad case of emphysema. And suppose also he has a strong addiction to smoking cigarettes. The doctor tells her that if he does not stop smoking around her she will die within the year (suppose the emphysema is a type which progresses unusually quickly). Now if he continues to smoke he would not be intentionally killing his

---

16. However, if the act is against Catholic teaching—papal teaching seems to assume or hold that every direct abortion is a direct killing (cf. John Paul II, *Evangelium Vitae* [The Gospel of Life] no. 58)—then I would advise anyone to follow Church teaching rather than what my philosophical conclusions might imply. There may very well be reasons against such an action which I have been unable to uncover.

wife. Her death would be only a side effect of his smoking in order to relax, relieve his discomfort, and so on. But, clearly, his continuing to smoke would be morally wrong. He might try to defend his action by saying that he is doing it not to kill her, but to avoid the misery of quitting smoking, to avoid the nervousness and agitation he suffers when he doesn't smoke. But the natural reply to this would be that the harms he would suffer from not smoking are beyond comparison with the harm his wife would suffer as a result of his continuing to smoke. How could he reasonably prefer his own comfort and relaxation to his wife's life?

Or suppose that instead of having to give up smoking, a man is asked to give up the use of certain chemicals necessary for his line of work. Suppose that he must work at his home (the cost of renting a shop is prohibitive). He is a photographic printer, and some of the chemicals he uses are killing his two-year-old child. Although his work has not made them rich (otherwise he could afford an outside shop), he does acquire real artistic fulfillment from it. If he does not use these chemicals, he simply must get another career. He tells his wife he is sorry but their child will just have to die, because he will not change his career.[17] Here also we would say that his changing careers is not comparable to a child's death. Even though in both actions there is a harm to a real and basic human good, still, the fact that shifting careers is not as total and irreparable a loss as death makes the action unjust or unfair. The fact that he has a real duty to his child is a relevant point also.

These examples show, first of all, that not all instances of causing a bad side effect are morally right. Also, they show that one of the important points to consider is the reason why the action which causes the bad side effect is chosen. If the reason

17. Or: suppose there are people who will adopt the child, but there is a nine-month waiting period. The husband refuses to change jobs for that period of time also, on the grounds that this will put him at a competitive disadvantage with respect to other photographic printers.

for choosing that action is a serious one, then perhaps causing the bad side effect is morally right. But if the reason is not weighty, or is not weighty when compared with the bad side effect, then the choice is unfair or unjust. Suppose the reason the action which causes the bad side effect is chosen is to avoid some harm, for that is the case in those abortions which are not intentional killing. Then, an important question is, is the harm one is avoiding by performing this action comparable to the harm which the action will cause as a side effect? The reason why continuing to smoke in the first example is so clearly immoral is that the harm avoided (discomfort) is not comparable, is not in the same category, with the harm caused (death). But abortion in a case where the mother's life is not significantly in danger is similar in the relevant respects. The harm avoided by the woman seeking the abortion is not comparable with the death caused to the child aborted. (Recall that the burden need only involve nine months of pregnancy; the woman can put the child up for adoption if necessary.)

In the vast majority of abortion cases, the man and woman freely perform an action, sexual intercourse, which they realize could result in the conception of a new human being.[18] Thus, most pregnancy cases are different from simply finding that someone is dependent on one for his or her life. Rather, they are cases of having put someone in a position of being dependent on one for his or her life. Parents have a special duty to their children, partly because they have performed an action which they fully realized could result in the procreation of children.

Thomson argues that one does not have a special responsibility to a child one conceives if one has taken measures to avoid conception.[19] The example she uses to illustrate her point is

18. Cf. Francis J. Beckwith, "Personal Bodily Rights, Abortion, and Unplugging the Violinist," *International Philosophical Quarterly* 32 (1992): 105–18.

19. In fact, she argues that one can have special responsibilities to someone

misleading. She writes: "If the room is stuffy, and I therefore open a window to air it, and a burglar climbs in, it would be absurd to say, 'Ah, now he can stay, she's given him a right to use her house—for she is partially responsible for his presence there, having voluntarily done what enabled him to get in, in full knowledge that there are such things as burglars, and that burglars burgle.'"[20] The analogy does not hold, for the woman's action does not cause the burglar to be in the house but only removes an obstacle; the burglar himself is the primary agent responsible for his being in the house. In the voluntary pregnancy case, however, the baby does not cause his or her presence in the mother's womb; rather, the mother and the father do.

Parents have a duty or responsibility to their children even if they have taken careful precautions to avoid having children, by contraception or by natural family planning. For, most people realize that contraceptives and other methods of avoiding conception have a certain rate of failure. Similarly, drunk drivers are responsible for damage they cause even if they make great efforts to avoid it. If the baseball I bat breaks my neighbor's window, I still have a responsibility to compensate my neighbor (fix the window) even though I tried very hard to bat the baseball in the opposite direction. Thus, contrary to Thomson's argument, we *are* responsible for the natural and foreseen results of our actions even if we try to avoid them.

---

only if one has voluntarily assumed them. But this is clearly mistaken. Counterexamples spring readily to mind. One has special responsibilities to one's parents, responsibilities one could scarcely foresee when accepting their care as a child. Would Thomson's argument justify abandoning one's old and feeble parents in the woods, as some people do with unwanted pets? We recognize that if someone finds himself or herself in a special circumstance where he or she alone can provide someone with help that person desperately needs, then he or she acquires simply by being in those circumstances a special responsibility.

20. Thomson, "A Defense," 182.

The responsibility to the child that stems from the fact that one has performed the action which causes the child's conception is a responsibility that belongs both to the mother and to the father. Our laws for child support recognize this point: fathers delinquent on their child support cannot rightly claim they have no duties to their children on the grounds that they wished not to have them. Thus, the parents of the child have a specific duty to the child. In virtue of that duty, the parents are morally required at least to refrain from performing an action that would cause the child's death.

iv. Abortion in Pregnancies Due to Rape

The case of abortion in a pregnancy due to rape needs to be discussed separately, for unlike the other cases, the woman has not voluntarily performed an action which she knows could result in a child. I limit the discussion to those cases in which what is intended is the ending of the condition of pregnancy, with the memories it evokes, and where the death of the child is a side effect. As mentioned, in a rape case there could be displaced emotions of revenge and hatred, but clearly, it is morally wrong intentionally to kill out of (displaced) revenge or hatred.

As the popularity of appeals to rape cases in arguments about abortion shows, the situation evokes our emotions and sometimes makes discussion difficult. As John Noonan notes, "Rape arouses fear and a desire for revenge, and reference to rape evokes emotion. The emotion has been enough for the state to take the life of the rapist. Horror of the crime is easily extended to horror of the product, so that the fetal life becomes forfeit too."[21]

The first point to make, and Noonan alludes to it, is that the

21. John Noonan, "How to Argue About Abortion," in *Morality in Practice,* ed. James Sterba, 2d ed. (Belmont, Cal.: Wadsworth, 1988), 151.

unborn child is not the one who committed the violence. The unborn child is innocent, and is moving and growing in a way that is simply natural for him or her. The child came to be through a violent act, but that is now irrelevant for how the child himself or herself should be treated. That is, the child deserves no less consideration on the grounds that he or she came to be through a horrible and violent act of his or her father.

But it is true that, unlike in other cases, the woman has not voluntarily placed the child in that imperiled condition. One might therefore say that the woman has less responsibility to this child than in other types of pregnancy. This may be a relevant consideration when she considers whether to give the child up for adoption, but it does not warrant performing an action which would cause the child's death. Granted that it is extremely difficult for a woman or girl pregnant after a rape to carry the baby to term, still, that difficulty is not in the same category as the harm that would be done to the child by causing his or her death. The difficulty for the mother which is unique to the pregnancy due to rape is the emotional distress she suffers by being reminded of the rape. But that emotional distress occasioned by the actual condition of pregnancy is temporary. The distress which would continue afterwards would exist in any case, and it can be alleviated or helped other than by causing the child's death. Moreover, as I will discuss below, it is far from clear that the abortion will help that emotional distress. The fundamental question is, is it morally right to do something that causes someone's death in order possibly to alleviate one's emotional distress? The answer to that question is clear: it is unjust to cause a person's death in that situation.

Moreover, the decisiveness of the innocence of the unborn child has not always been appreciated. Expelling the child from the womb at an early stage of pregnancy imposes a grave burden on the child, since it causes his or her death. Now, the fact that the woman has been violated does not morally justify her imposing such a burden on an innocent third party. Suppose someone illegally dumped garbage into my yard. May I then rake the garbage into my innocent neighbor's yard? Or may I pass counterfeit money to an innocent party because I innocently received it myself? No, in both cases. Michael Davis expresses the principle involved in such cases, as well as in the case of pregnancy due to rape, as follows: "That one has been wronged does not make permissible imposing on one who did not do the wrong (and was not otherwise to blame for it) burdens it would otherwise be impermissible to impose on him."[22] To expel the child from the womb and thus cause his or her death is thus to shift a burden wrongly imposed on one to an innocent third party, and is therefore unjust.

Furthermore, even though the woman has not voluntarily performed the action which causes the child's conception, the biological relationship itself does have moral significance. Although she did not choose to conceive, or even consent to the act which caused the conception, the child is from her, or of her. It is wrong to say that the fetus is merely a part of the woman's body, for the child is a distinct organism; nevertheless, this claim is not totally groundless. The relationship is one of physical continuity or prolongation. There is a unique physical unity or continuity of children to their parents. The child is brought into being out of the very genes of the mother and the father. The mother and the father are in a certain sense prolonged or continued in their progeny.

This point—difficult to articulate, but something most people have a certainty of on the common sense level—has two important implications for the morality of abortion in pregnancies due to rape. First, this physical bond creates a special duty to the child. Second, and perhaps more clearly, an action chosen by the mother which kills this child is an action against herself, against herself because she exists in a way in her child.

22. Michael Davis, "Foetuses, Famous Violinists, and the Right to Continued Aid," *Philosophical Quarterly* 33 (1983): 268.

This second implication has important psychological ramifications for pregnancies due to rape. The central violation in rape is a loss of autonomy.[23] Along with this often comes a loss of self-esteem. The rape victim needs to sense her regaining of autonomy, and to regain her self-esteem.[24] But insofar as causing the death of her child is an attack on herself, or on the prolongation of herself, to that extent abortion prolongs rather than helps the violation involved in rape.

Thus, it is important to see that abortion is unlikely to help the emotional condition of a woman or girl trying to recover from the horrible violence of rape. From all accounts, both pro- and antiabortion, abortion is itself a highly traumatic experience.[25] The awareness that one has killed a developing life within one is not an awareness that coheres well with the rest of the psyche in most girls or women. Many times that awareness comes back to haunt them, causing them severe emotional problems, and it is more likely to do so the more serious the

23. Cf. Mary Catherine Sommers, "Living Together: Burdensome Pregnancy and the Hospitable Self," in *Catholicism and Abortion,* ed. Stephen Heaney (Braintree, Mass.: Pope John Center, 1992), 243–64.

24. On this point see Sandra Kathleen Mahkorn and William Dolan, "Pregnancy and Sexual Assault," in *New Perspectives on Human Abortion,* ed. Thomas Hilgers, Dennis Horan, and David Mall (Frederick, Md.: University Publications of America, 1981), 182–98; and David Reardon, *Aborted Women: Silent No More* (Chicago: Loyola University Press, 1987), 188–219.

25. For examples, see Kathleen McDonnell, *Not an Easy Choice: A Feminist Re-examines Abortion* (Boston: South End Press, 1984); James Burtchaell, *Rachel Weeping and Other Essays on Abortion* (New York: Andrews and McMeel, 1982), 1–60; Paula Ervin, *Women Exploited: The Other Victims of Abortion* (Huntington, In.: Our Sunday Visitor, 1985); Nancy Michels, *Helping Women Recover from Abortion* (Minneapolis: Bethany House, 1988); C. L. Tischler, "Adolescent Suicide Attempts Following Elective Abortion: A Special Case of Anniversary Reaction," *Pediatrics* 68 (1990): 670–71; G. Ney, "Mental Health and Abortion: Review and Analysis," *Psychiatric Journal of the University of Ottawa* 14 (1989): 513–15; and E. Joanne Angelo, "Psychiatric Sequelae of Abortion: The Many Faces of Post-Abortion Grief," *Linacre Quarterly* 59 (1992): 69–80.

reason was to have the abortion.[26] That is, women with the smallest chance of having severe emotional problems through feeling guilt about an abortion are those who had abortions for trivial reasons. The more serious the motive, that is, the more pressure there was to choose abortion, the more likely they will have serious emotional problems later. This means that girls or women who have abortions in pregnancies due to rape— though the number is quite small—are the most likely to have emotional problems later.[27]

In other words, in addition to the injustice to the unborn child, having the abortion is more likely to exacerbate the mental and emotional problems of the girl or woman pregnant due to rape. For these reasons, rape cases do not provide moral grounds for abortion.

In sum, most abortions are intentional killing. Of those that are not intentional killing, if the woman's life is significantly in danger, I have no philosophical argument to show that causing the child's death as a side effect would never be morally justified. If the woman's life is not in danger, and the sexual intercourse was voluntary, then causing the child's death is not justified, since (1) the woman (and the man) caused the child to be in that dependent condition, and (2) the harm caused is significantly worse than the harm avoided. If the woman's life is not significantly endangered, but the pregnancy is due to rape, (1) does not apply. But abortion in that case is still not justified because of (2), and because (3) causing the child's death by abortion unfairly shifts a burden to an innocent third party, (4) the child is still her child, and (5) aborting the child is likely to exacerbate the woman's emotional and psychological condition rather than help it.

26. Cf. Reardon, *Aborted Women*, chaps. 4–6.
27. Ibid. See also Mahkorn and Dolan, "Pregnancy and Sexual Assault."

v. Is the Fetus Merely Deprived of What He or She Had No Right To?

F. M. Kamm has recently developed Judith Thomson's argument, adding a significant new step. She argues that abortion is justified because the fetus loses only the life that is provided by the woman's support, a support the woman was not morally obliged to begin giving, and the fetus is as a result no worse off than the fetus would have been if he or she had not been conceived. Kamm writes:

We need not deny that we harm the fetus in killing it relative to the condition it would have been in if the woman continued support. But it may not be wrong to harm it in this way, because we may be obliged only not to harm it relative to the condition it would have been in if it had not been attached. If the woman has no duty to aid it because of its need or other grounds of special obligation, any condition it is in as a result of her support is not something it has a claim to keep, at least as long as it continues to need her support to maintain it.[28]

On Kamm's argument, then, the woman has only withdrawn what she was not required to provide.[29]

The decisive difficulty in this argument is that it supposes that the fetus, or child, has been caused to be in a condition identical to what it would have been in minus the woman's life-supporting activities. But this assumption is mistaken. If the woman had never provided support to the fetus, then the fetus would never have been. If she aborts the fetus, however, the fetus first lives and then dies.[30] Although being dead may not

28. F. M. Kamm, *Creation and Abortion: A Study in Moral and Legal Philosophy* (New York: Oxford University Press, 1992), 80.

29. She also argues that the woman may intentionally kill the child as a means to withdrawing burdensome support. However, if the first part of her argument does not succeed, as I will argue, then this additional claim is without support, and so need not be considered here.

30. Cf. Davis, "The Right to Continued Aid," 259–78, esp. 273–78.

be a "condition," we cannot morally equate depriving someone of life—even if they do not anticipate that deprivation (say,
killing them in their sleep)—with never having been. So, her
action causes the fetus to lose his or her life, which is quite
different from never having been.

The coming to be of a child is unique. There are analogies
for it, but every analogy severely limps. The situation here is
that the woman, and the father, do give the child a benefit in
causing his or her coming to be; the beginning of his or her
life is a benefit received from his or her parents. But at the same
time the bestowal of this benefit places the child in a dependent
and imperiled condition, and so the bestowal of this benefit also
creates a responsibility on the part of the mother and the father.
If the child existed prior to the mother's life-supporting actions,
and the mother simply withdrew support from the child and
left him or her in the condition in which he or she would have
been had the woman's actions not affected the child's life at
all—if this were an accurate description of the situation, then
Kamm's argument would have a point. But it is not an accurate
description. Rather, the child comes to be as dependent on the
mother, and so, contrary to Kamm's analysis, no one can now
cause the child to be as he or she would have been minus the
woman's support. Being dead is not the same as never having
been; otherwise, not procreating would be equivalent to killing. Being deprived of life by someone from whom I received
life is still being deprived of life and thus being seriously
harmed.

VI. The Famous Violinist

Perhaps the most persuasive feature of Thomson's argument
is her analogy concerning the famous violinist with kidney disease. It would be right, she claims, to unplug the violinist from
your kidneys even though this would cause his death; in many
cases abortion is similar in the relevant respects; therefore, in

many cases abortion is morally right. But *are* the two cases in fact similar in the relevant respects, or are there relevant dissimilarities between the two?

Thomson relies on our intuitions telling us that it would be morally right to unplug the violinist. But I believe that the more the circumstances of the violinist case are made similar to a pregnancy case, the more likely we are to see or feel that it would *not* be morally right to unplug the violinist. There are several circumstances peculiar to the violinist case, that is, circumstances not matched by anything comparable in a pregnancy case, that pull our intuitions, so to speak, toward approving unplugging. First, the violinist was plugged into you by an act of violence and injustice. Something comparable, but not exactly so, exists in pregnancies due to rape, but only in those. Moreover, even in a pregnancy due to rape the situation is not as similar as it may first appear. When imagining the situation one cannot help but think of the violinist as part of the plan to become hooked up to you. In a pregnancy due to rape the child has absolutely no part in the attack, but is an innocent result of the attack.

Second, as mentioned above, the violinist has not been placed in a condition worse than what he would have been in minus your support, whereas this cannot be said of the unborn child. In the violinist case it may be plausible to describe your action as not-giving-aid, whereas abortions cannot be accurately described in that way. To return the child to the condition he or she was in previous to one's actions one would have to bring it about that the child never was—an impossible task. Instead, in most abortions the parents first cause the child to be and to be in an imperiled and dependent condition, and then perform an action that kills the child.[31] In abortions due to rape, the woman

---

31. Suppose you first consented to the violinist being hooked up to you, and then changed your mind, meanwhile spoiling his only chance to have someone else agree to the procedure. In such a case it seems clear the violinist

unfairly shifts the burden of a wrong done to her onto the child, an innocent bystander in this case.

Third, the burden of being hooked up to the violinist is considerably greater than pregnancy. Thomson begins the case talking of being hooked up to the violinist for nine years, and only later brings it down to nine months, and then finally to nine hours (where she concedes it would be wrong to unplug him). Moreover, most significantly, if you are plugged into the violinist, you cannot carry on the rest of your life. As Rosalind Hursthouse observes, in the violinist example you are bedridden and in enforced communicating company with a stranger for a whole nine months. These burdens are not matched in the case of pregnancy. In the violinist example, she points out:

I cannot do my job, I cannot visit my sick mother, I cannot go to my sister's wedding, I cannot go to the films, I cannot go swimming, I cannot read (well, perhaps the violinist is a great talker), I cannot have a confidential conversation with anyone and I cannot make love. And all of this for a whole nine months. But the usual pregnancy does not make one bed-ridden, and even when it does, very rarely for nine months; nor is the foetus, even assuming it to be a person, someone whose presence rules out reading, private conversations, and sex.[32]

The cases Thomson compares to pregnancy as a basis for her argument have significant dissimilarities. Indeed, it is precisely the features unique to the violinist example—the injustice and the extensive burdens—that pull on our intuitions so that we tend to feel it would certainly be permissible to unhook the violinist.[33]

---

has been harmed, because your deciding to give him aid or your beginning to give him aid and then your subsequent withdrawal of it has left him worse off than had you not begun the aid to begin with. See Davis, "The Right to Continued Aid." This case is more nearly analogous to most abortion cases than is Thomson's violinist case.

32. Rosalind Hursthouse, *Beginning Lives* (New York: Oxford University Press, 1988), 203.

33. Cf. Michael Wreen, "Abortion and Pregnancy Due to Rape," *Phi-*

VII. The Unborn Child as an Aggressor?

An argument touched on by Judith Jarvis Thomson, although not developed by her, is that it is morally right to kill the child because it is right to kill an aggressor, and the unborn child is an aggressor. On this view, the unborn child has lost his or her right to life because he or she is an unjust aggressor, and so it is permissible to kill the child, even though one's life may not be endangered.

However, Baruch Brody has clearly shown that the fetus cannot be categorized as an "aggressor." An aggressor need not be *guilty* of his threat in order to be an aggressor, but at the very least there must be some action which he is performing, and which he would be guilty of if he did it voluntarily, in order for him to be correctly classified as an "aggressor."[34] If five of us are on a lifeboat stranded at sea, and we realize it is sinking and it will hold only four, I cannot reasonably view the others as "aggressors" even though their continued existence threatens me. I cannot view even the one who last entered the boat as an "aggressor," for the action of entering the boat is not reasonably viewed as a pursuit against my life. It is not something he would be guilty of if he did it voluntarily; it is not an action that is in any way *aimed* at my life or well-being. And this is the principal reason why the fetus cannot be classified as an aggressor, unjust or otherwise. The fetus is simply growing and developing in a way quite natural to him or her; the fetus is not performing any action that could in any way be construed as aimed at the life or well-being of the mother.

If it did turn out that there were situations where it is morally right for the child to be removed from the womb—aborted— to save the life of the mother (but see note 16 above), the justification of those actions would not be that the fetus is an ag-

---

losophia 21 (1992): 201–20; and Schwarz, *The Moral Question of Abortion,* 113–24.

34. Baruch Brody, *Abortion and the Sanctity of Human Life* (Cambridge: MIT Press, 1975), 6–12.

gressor, but that in those cases the death of the child would be a side effect of what is intended, and the harm caused the child, in those cases, comparable to the harm avoided. But such actions would be morally right only if another condition were met, namely, that the selection of which one to save were just.

5

Consequentialist Arguments

I argued in chapters 1 through 3 that abortion is the killing of a human person. In chapter 4 I argued that abortion is usually intentional killing, and that if it is not, it is still morally wrong except perhaps in some cases in which it is done to save the mother's life. One might grant, however, that abortion is the intentional killing of a human person, but still hold that sometimes it is morally right, as a means to avoid bad consequences. Almost all moral theories hold that it is at least *prima facie* wrong intentionally to kill innocent persons. So, if one holds that it is in this or that case morally right, there must be some overriding reason. Usually the overriding reason consists in an appeal to consequences. So, although not every theory which denies it is always wrong intentionally to kill the innocent is consequentialist or utilitarian in its whole approach, still, the particular argument to justify intentionally killing the innocent is most likely to be consequentialist in its structure.

Consequentialist arguments for abortion are more frequently presented in popular circles than in philosophical ones.[1] When actual participants in abortion are asked about their reasons for choosing abortion, and about the morality of abortion itself, they frequently present consequentialist arguments. Thus, discussing her experience of abortion, a newspaper columnist who defends abortion wrote:

> About the question "Does life begin at conception?"—I don't know. Life in a certain sense probably does begin at conception, even perhaps right before conception—the properties of life are in the sperm and they're in the womb. But one must make tough choices in this world, harder choices than abortion.[2]

The suggestion is that even if abortion is the intentional killing of a human person—though there is hesitation to grant that point—it is sometimes justified as a means of avoiding very bad consequences.

1. A Variety of Consequentialisms

In recent years the discussion of consequentialism has become extraordinarily complicated. A definitive examination of

1. In philosophical journals the merits of consequentialism itself are more often discussed. Indeed, consequentialist cases for specific conclusions are seldom presented, with the exception of capital punishment.

2. From *The Choices We Made: Twenty-Five Women Speak Out About Abortion*, ed. Angela Bonvoglia (New York: Random House, 1991), 87. Similarly, telling her story of abortion, an actress wrote, "Abortion might be killing a life; I don't know. That to me is not an issue. If there is a sin, it is the sin that we adults perpetrate on the children of the earth who truly are innocent and defenseless by bringing those children into the world when they will not be cared for" (99). Another successful actress wrote: "I had that abortion because I viewed having a child at that time as an end to my life. All of my hopes and dreams for myself would have had to be put aside. I had planned and worked hard all my life to be an actress" (105).

consequentialism would require a more extensive treatment than I am able to give in this work. I will try here to set out some reasons which suggest that this approach has shortcomings. The consequentialist argument can be interpreted in various ways, because there are several types of consequentialism. The first distinction is that between egoistic consequentialism and utilitarianism.[3] Both hold that an action is right if and only if it produces the best (or least bad) consequences. They differ on what consequences they consider significant. For the egoistic consequentialist the only significant ones are those which happen to oneself, whereas for the utilitarian the consequences for everyone, not just those for oneself, must be counted. Few people defend egoistic consequentialism. In chapter 2 I argued that the goods one recognizes as intrinsically good are aspects of human fulfillment, and are recognized as good and worthy of pursuit not just as they can be instantiated in oneself but also as they can be in others. Thus, egoism is mistaken. I will therefore concentrate in the rest of this chapter on utilitarianism, that is, nonegoistic consequentialist arguments.

There are several types of utilitarianism. The utilitarian may identify the good consequences as consisting in pleasure (hedonistic utilitarianism), or in the satisfaction of preferences (preference utilitarianism), or in various perfections or fulfillments of human beings, that is, in basic goods conceived along the line I argued for in chapter 2 (ideal utilitarianism). I argued in chapter 2 that the intrinsic goods which in some way constitute a standard for morally good action (although how they do so is at issue between utilitarians and nonutilitarians) are not to be identified with pleasure or the satisfaction of the desires people happen to have. What is intrinsically good is what really perfects or fulfills a human person, not just an experience or what happens to be desired. Because ideal utilitarianism is

3. Cf. William Frankena, *Ethics* (Englewood Cliffs, N.J.: Prentice-Hall, 1973), chap. 3, for this terminology.

the most plausible form of utilitarianism, I will refer to it most frequently. Nevertheless, the arguments presented here apply equally to any type of utilitarianism.

There are still further differences within utilitarianism concerning (1) how various distributions of the good and bad consequences should matter and (2) which subjects' good and bad consequences should be considered. Regarding distributions, "Act so as to produce the best (or least bad) consequences in the long run," or "maximize the good," may mean that one should produce the sheer largest amount of good (or sheer least amount of bad), regardless of how the good and the bad are distributed. Or, instead of referring to *total* happiness or welfare, the principle could mean that one should maximize the *average* happiness or welfare of people or of those affected by one's action. Or, again, it could be interpreted as prescribing that option which will produce the best consequences for the least well off in society, an option called "maximin."

Regarding which subjects to consider, as John Bigelow and Robert Pargetter have pointed out, it makes a difference whether one includes possible but nonactual persons in the group who will be recipients of the consequences of one's action, or only actual people.[4] They argue as follows:

Suppose you settle on average happiness. There seems something unsatisfactory about making a better world by leaving the happiness of those in the world untouched and simply adding some more people with a happiness level above average. Even if there is some degree of merit in raising the average by that means, it is not morally on a par with, say, cheering up everyone equally. Or if we settle on total, rather than average happiness, surely just having a machine producing slightly happy beings and leaving the happiness levels of all the existing inhabitants of the world the same is not on a par with improving the total happiness by improving the lives of some of the existing inhabitants.[5]

4. John Bigelow and Robert Pargetter, "Morality, Potential Persons and Abortion," *American Philosophical Quarterly* 25 (1988): 173–81.

5. Ibid., 179–80.

Whether their comparative value-judgments are right is another matter, but Bigelow and Pargetter illustrate the important differences among utilitarians. So far, then, there are six types of utilitarianisms, with different maximal goals:

1. total happiness for both possible and actual subjects;
2. total happiness for actual subjects;
3. average happiness for both possible and actual subjects;
4. average happiness for actual subjects;
5. maximin for both possible and actual subjects; and
6. maximin for actual subjects.

There seem to be serious difficulties with each of these candidates. With (1) and (2) it would seem to be not only morally permissible, but morally required, to enslave a minority if their unhappiness or deprivations would be counterbalanced by the increased happiness or welfare of the majority (whether of actual persons or of both actual and nonactual but possible persons). With (3) and (4) it seems that enslavement of a minority could, in some circumstances, raise the average happiness, even though it would decidedly lower the happiness of the enslaved minority. (2) and (4) seem to have this difficulty, that they would allow or perhaps require this generation simply to use up all of the world's resources in such a way that there would be no future generations.[6] (1) and (3) seem to have the difficulties Bigelow and Pargetter indicate, and also seem to imply that, so far as what is primarily to be considered in an action, failing to produce a child (through celibacy, natural family planning, or contraception) would be morally on a par with killing a child who already exists.[7] Moreover, it seems that it would be morally obligatory with (1) and (3) to produce more children each time it became clear (if it could become clear)

6. Cf. John Finnis, *Natural Law and Natural Rights* (Oxford: Clarendon Press, 1980), 117–18.

7. Side effects of killing a child could be argued by utilitarians to make it worse, generally, than not producing a child to begin with. But the difference between killing and not producing certainly seems to be greater than that.

that the child produced would have, in his or her lifetime, a net positive amount of happiness or welfare.[8] Similar difficulties arise with the alternatives labeled "maximin."

Of course, proponents of these theories will perhaps amend them, in order to resolve such difficulties. The point I wish to make in this section, however, is that there is an ineradicable indeterminacy in utilitarianism. There is no nonarbitrary way of removing the indeterminacies mentioned above. There is no utilitarian way to settle whether only actual persons should count or possible persons should count as well, or which distribution should be preferred. But a moral theory which is ineradicably indeterminate cannot reasonably provide moral guidance. Utilitarianism or consequentialism, then, does not seem to offer a standard by which to guide one's actions. Rather, it offers a general idea, but an idea which remains indeterminate enough to allow conflicting judgments.

II. Utilitarianism and Justice

The second difficulty in utilitarianism is that, as many have argued, it conflicts with justice. More precisely, utilitarianism seems to require the performance of clearly unjust acts. I say that utilitarianism *seems to* require the performance of such actions because, as I have noted, the principle is indeterminate and therefore it is always possible for a utilitarian to reach a conclusion opposite what it may seem utilitarianism requires.

A frequently discussed example is a sheriff in a small town. McCloskey writes:

Suppose that a sheriff were faced with the choice either of framing a Negro for a rape that had aroused hostility to the Negroes (a particular Negro generally being believed to be guilty but whom the sheriff knows not to be guilty)—and thus preventing serious

8. Some would argue, though, that such happiness was counterbalanced by unhappiness caused to those responsible for the child.

anti-Negro riots which would probably lead to some loss of life and increased hatred of each other by whites and Negroes—or of hunting for the guilty person and thereby allowing the anti-Negro riots to occur, while doing the best he can to combat them.[9]

McCloskey argues that if the sheriff were a utilitarian, then he would commit judicial murder, since it would seem to produce the lesser evil here. But we know that judicial murder is wrong. Therefore, utilitarianism is mistaken.

Of course, the utilitarian could stand fast to his principle and claim that such a killing would indeed be morally right.[10] So the argument only appeals to those who see that the concrete implications of utilitarianism are wrong, and who have more trust in this conviction than in whatever appeal the principle proposed by utilitarianism might have for them. Still, the argument does present a definite difficulty.

Russell Hardin has argued that such counterexamples to utilitarianism are far-fetched, based only on supposing the world to be very different than the way it is.[11] But this objection is specious. Not only do such examples seem quite realistic, but events similar to them in the relevant respects have frequently occurred.

A second example, again entirely possible, is cited by Robert Munson in his anthology on medical ethics. He asks us to imagine an experimenter who wishes to learn about the functioning of the brain. He could do so most effectively by systematically destroying the brain of one person, noting the results. Such a study, we could imagine, would help countless numbers of people in very significant ways, although it would

9. H. J. McCloskey, "An Examination of Restricted Utilitarianism," in *Studies in Utilitarianism,* ed. Thomas K. Hearn (New York: Appleton-Century-Crofts, 1971), 234.

10. See J. J. C. Smart and B. A. O. Williams, *Utilitarianism: For and Against* (Cambridge: Cambridge University Press, 1973).

11. Russell Hardin, *Morality Within the Limits of Reason* (Chicago: University of Chicago Press, 1988), 23–25.

involve immense suffering in one. Would not the utilitarian conclude that the suffering of the one would be outweighed by the happiness resulting for the many?[12]

These examples show that utilitarianism seems to prescribe actions which we know to be immoral, and thus it must be mistaken. Moreover, this difficulty regarding justice is especially acute in the case of abortion. Utilitarian arguments for abortion claim that the death of the child is outweighed by the benefit to the many. But such a claim is far from plausible when made about mature human beings in other contexts, such as judicial murder or medical experiments.

III. Incommensurability of Options for Free Choice

A third difficulty in utilitarianism concerns the measurement of the consequences. How can one measure the goodness and badness of the consequences of different actions against one another? Consider the case of an unmarried high school girl who discovers that she is pregnant. She considers the options of having the child and giving him or her up for adoption or having an abortion. Suppose her friends encourage her to have the abortion, on the grounds that "it will be better for all concerned." On what basis could her friends reach that judgment? They would have to determine, first, what the consequences of having the child would be, both good and bad, then, what the consequences of aborting would be, both good and bad, and, finally, somehow measure the goodness or badness of the first option against the goodness or badness of the second option, to reach the judgment that the net goodness or badness of one option is greater than that of the other. Suppose her friends reason that if she does not have the abortion, she will be forced

12. Ronald Munson, *Intervention and Reflection: Basic Issues in Medical Ethics,* 4th ed. (Belmont, Cal.: Wadsworth, 1992), 10.

to change schools, her education will suffer, and her relationship with her parents will suffer. These terrible evils, they argue, outweigh whatever immediate harm may be done to the unborn.

The reasoning, however, is faulty. It would be sound only if one could measure harms to the goods of education and parental friendship[13] on the one hand, against a death and a choice to cause that death,[14] on the other hand. But how can education or friendship be objectively measured against life and respect for life? Moreover, in killing the child, one not only deprives that person of life but also of all the goods of that person which depend on life. But how can education or friendship be objectively measured against life and respect for life? By what objective criterion does one say that instances of some goods are better or worse than instances of other goods?[15] A similar problem will occur in any morally significant choice. In every significant choice various basic goods will be at stake—one or more type(s) of good instantiated in this option, and others in the other option—and so one will not be able to measure objectively the options for choice against one another.[16]

Two things can be measured against one another only if they

13. Of course, one may reasonably doubt that a relationship with one's parents would be aided by killing a child in order to hide past wrong-doings or mistakes from them.

14. The choice to cause the death is something bad in addition to the death itself.

15. As we shall see, the problem is not confined to different types of good, but also extends to different instances of the same good, for example, two lives. Usually, however, different types of good are involved in the options for choice, and in such cases the problem we are discussing is particularly clear.

16. Arguments of this type against consequentialism were developed in detail by Germain Grisez, Joseph Boyle, and, later, John Finnis. See Germain Grisez, Joseph Boyle, and John Finnis, *Nuclear Deterrence, Morality and Realism* (New York: Oxford University Press, 1987), 238–74; and Germain Grisez, Joseph Boyle, and John Finnis, "Practical Principles, Moral Truth, and Ultimate Ends," *American Journal of Jurisprudence* 32 (1987): 99–151.

have some property in common, and one can say of one that it has more of that property than does the other. One can say that A is longer than B only if length or time is held in common by both. A is hotter than B only if both have temperature or heat in common. The property may be inherent in the items compared, or it may be a relational property, for example, the effectiveness for bringing about or contributing to a certain goal.

One can say that A is *better* than B only with respect to some standard which can be applied to both. For to say that A is *good* is not to describe it, but simply to say that A fulfills the standards of the kind of things it is. "Good" expresses a supervenient predicate, that is, one calls something "good" in virtue of its having certain other properties which make it fulfill some standard one applies to the things of that sort.[17] So, I cannot meaningfully say that A is good without having in mind some way of answering the question, "good what," "good in what respect?" A, for example, may be a very good football player, a very good carpenter, but a not-so-good student, or a not-so-good father. In that case, to say that A is "good," without specifying good *what,* is empty. Therefore, to say meaningfully that one thing is *better* than another, one must be able to specify in what respect (or respects) A is better than B. But, again, in every significant choice various basic goods are at stake, and so there is no way one can say that one option is better in every respect than the others.

Garth Hallett argues that the common property needed for objective comparison might be simply *value.* That is, Hallett holds that the options do have a common property and the property is value. After considering Grisez's claim that options for choice are incommensurable because they lack a common property, Hallett writes:

An obvious rejoinder is: what about value? The requisite 'common denominator' need not be a single goal or purpose; it may be a

17. Cf. John Campbell and Robert Pargetter, "Goodness and Fragility," *American Philosophical Quarterly* 23 (1986): 155–65.

single feature or aspect with respect to which various things are compared as more or less. . . . If it be asked in what respect varied values are comparable, the natural answer would seem to be: with respect to value. After all, why are they all called values—by Grisez as by others—if they are not similar at least in this respect? Thus, as the common denominator of weights, permitting comparison, is weight, and the common denominator of pains, permitting comparison, is pain, and so forth, so (a proportionalist would say) the common denominator of values, permitting comparison, is value. What else?[18]

The difficulty is that Hallett is treating the term "value" as if it were a first level predicate, whereas it is, as I have said, a supervenient predicate. "Good" expresses completeness or fulfillment or perfection with respect to some standard.[19] "Value"

18. Garth Hallett, "The 'Incommensurability' of Values," *Heythrop Journal* 28 (1987): 376.

19. Goodness is quite different from, say, redness. "Red," said of a sweater and of a fire truck, denotes a quality held in common by those two very different things. To know what it is like for a sweater to be red is the same as knowing what it is like for a fire truck to be red, because once one has grasped what the quality is, then it is just a matter of different applications—the feature which makes the sweater red is specifically the same as the feature which makes the fire truck red.

But the situation is quite different with goodness. To know what it is like for a book to be good is not the same as to know what it is like for a person to be good, or for a horse to be good, or so on. The features which make the book good are quite different from the features which make the person good. On the other hand, the way in which a book is good is not just unrelated to the way in which a person is good. In other words, one cannot say that "good" must denote a quality in one case (e.g., as said of a person) and has meaning in the more complex way noted above in all other cases. "Good" as said of a book and of a person (and of a size, of a horse, and so on) is predicated not equivocally (where the meanings are unrelated), but analogically (the meanings, while different, have a determinate relation). All of this indicates that "good" expresses a different sort of concept—not the concept of a quality, but a more complex concept. The concepts are composites of a constant schema and variable contents. The constant schema is the fulfillment or perfection of a thing, which is to say, it is meeting some standard. The varying contents will be the features in the things which constitute their ful-

and "good" are synonyms, or at least near synonyms; so, one has value, or is good, only by having some other property or properties in virtue of which one fulfills a standard. Value is not itself a property of which one has more or less. And so it cannot be the common denominator Hallett claims it to be.

Two things could be measured against one another if they had a common relation to a single end. In that case, even though A and B have nothing in common in themselves, they might have in common the fact that each is related to a goal C. In that case, if A is more efficient in helping one realize C, then one can meaningfully say that A is better than B, at least in *that* respect.

The common property, either inherent or relational, need not be quantifiable in the sense that one can assign numbers to the various instances of it. One can say that A is more red than B, or better with respect to the color red (a more saturated color), without being able to assign a numerical value to the greater intensity of color. Still, they are being compared in regard to their possession of a single property.[20]

A and B also can be compared in regard to possession of a single property when one of them lacks the property completely. In that case, of course, the one that does have the property excels the other. Thus, one can say that, ontologically, an

---

fillment of their standards, or which bring about some thing's fulfillment of standards.

Thus, to know what it is like for a book to be good is not the same as to know what it is like for a person to be good, because the book's fulfilling the standards for a book are not the same as a person's fulfilling the standards for a person. Yet, "good" said of a book is not just equivocal with "good" said of a person (which would be the case if "good" said of a person referred simply to a quality in that person), because there is a schema held in common by the two predications, namely, "good" does refer to the fulfilling of some standard—albeit a different standard in each case.

20. One could also say of two colors in photographs, for example, that, "This red is more saturated (a purer color, less diluted by other colors) than that blue." Even so, there is a common property, namely, color saturation.

animal is better than a plant, and a human being better than other animals, for an animal has positive properties which a plant lacks, and human beings have positive properties which other animals lack. (Moreover, all the potentialities of the lesser entity are possessed by the higher entity, and then some.)

Also, one could say that one thing is better than another with respect to two or more properties, provided that the better excels the other in every property, or provided that one determines that the one which excels the other in more properties is better (even though in many cases *that* determination may be quite tricky).

Now, the only thing that could function as a common property in either of these ways, that is, as a single goal distinct from the various basic goods instantiated in the options for choice and as a measure of them, would be human happiness or human perfection or flourishing. In some cases this property can function in the desired way. If A is an instance of an inherent human good and B is an instrumental good, then one can say that A is objectively better than B. Thus, one can say that a human life is objectively better than money, or a good appearance, for example. For in those cases human flourishing logically functions as a property distinct from the objects measured, and one object is seen as closer to the standard than others, because it is within or included in it while the others are outside it. But if A and B are both inherent human goods, then human perfection cannot accurately be treated as a single property. Human beings are complex entities and their perfection or flourishing is found in several categories. One cannot measure knowledge of truth, for example, against human life because they do not have a single property in common in relation to which one can say that one excels the other.

In other words, human happiness or flourishing cannot be the common property because it is simply the whole composed of knowledge of truth, life, and others as components. And there is no further goal beyond human happiness or flourishing the relation to which could serve as the common property or standard.[21] So: (1) there is no goal beyond the basic goods that function as the common property or single measuring standard; and (2) the goods in the options for choice do not themselves share a single property in common. Thus, it remains that the options for choice are incommensurable.

In sum, in every situation where one has a significant choice between options, there are different instances of basic human goods being affected in the options for choice, and so there always are different sorts of goods which would have to be compared and measured by the utilitarian. Thus, in significant choices there is no single standard by which to measure the goodness and badness found in options for choice, and so one cannot perform the type of measurement of consequences which utilitarianism requires.[22] Notice that I have discussed

21. A Christian might object that union with God could be construed as a goal beyond the basic goods which could serve as the standard for measuring them. This is not the case. There are two theological problems with this position. First, human perfection does not of itself bring one closer to union with God—to hold that it does would be the Pelagian heresy. Secondly, this view reduces participation in basic human goods, or human perfection, to mere means in relation to an end beyond them. This position is contrary to Vatican Council II, *The Constitution on the Church in the Modern World (Gaudium et Spes)*, nos. 34–39. The kingdom of God includes both communion with God, which is *supernatural,* as well as human perfection, including the bodily perfection of human beings. The basic goods are the natural components of the eternal kingdom, and so they are not merely extrinsically related to heaven; nor are they mere instruments in relation to divine communion, as the position behind this objection would lead to.

22. Thus we can see that one of the chief arguments in support of utilitarianism is based on an incoherence. It is often argued in support of utilitarianism that one should always prefer the greater good, or the lesser evil, for the only alternative is to say that in some cases one should prefer the lesser good or the greater evil. But the argument supposes that a clear sense can be given in this context to the phrases, "greater good," and "lesser evil." And if the consequences of actions, in a free choice, cannot really be measured against one another, then the phrases "greater good," "lesser evil," "greater evil," and so on, simply do not have sense.

two types of incommensurabilities: of basic goods, and of options for choice. In this first argument, I have used the first type of incommensurability to argue for the second type. The second type directly shows the unworkability of utilitarianism.

Another argument can be given to show that the options for choice are incommensurable. Germain Grisez has argued that utilitarianism implies that an immoral choice both could and could not be made.[23] As a moral theory, utilitarianism is presented as guidance for making morally significant choices, as a method for deciding what one ought to do in morally problematic situations. This implies that the one choosing is able to choose the morally bad alternative, that it is possible for one to make the wrong choice. But utilitarianism claims that one discovers the morally right choice by determining that one alternative offers objectively more good than the other alternative. And, Grisez argues, if one sees that one alternative offers more good, simply speaking, than the others, one could not choose—as a rationally motivated choice—any of the other alternatives.

If I see that one alternative offers as much good as the other alternatives and more, then the other alternatives simply drop out of consideration, that is, I have no reason for choosing the other alternatives. For example, if in trying to choose among houses to buy for my family I see that one is too small, costs more, and is in an inferior location compared to the other houses I've examined, that house simply drops out of consideration. In other words, I can choose an option only if it offers, or seems to offer, something distinctively attractive. For to choose an action is to will to perform an action for the sake of something good one thinks it participates in or will help one realize.

Robert McKim and Peter Simpson have objected to this ar-

23. Germain Grisez, "Against Consequentialism," *American Journal of Jurisprudence* 23 (1978): 21–72. See also works referenced in n. 16.

gument by claiming that it ignores the possibility that one might choose the lesser good through selfishness. They argue that it is possible for one to see which alternative offers the unqualifiedly greater good—which is to view the alternatives from the moral point of view, or the standpoint of impartial benevolence—and yet choose another alternative which is superior from the standpoint of selfishness. Speaking of Grisez's argument, they write, "But this reasoning is defective. It conflates weighing-all-goods with weighing-all-goods-from-all-points-of-view. The former is necessary for proportionalist [that is, utilitarian] calculation, but the latter is not, and is probably not even possible."[24]

Grisez, Boyle, and Finnis replied to this objection to their argument.[25] The objection could be taken in two ways. If emphasis is laid upon the ability to view the goods offered by the various alternatives from different points of view, then it turns out to be a nonobjection actually agreeing with the point made by the argument. For the point could be expressed this way: there is not just one standard or standpoint according to which one can measure the consequences against one another. If utilitarianism is a point of view from which one measures the goodness and badness of the consequences, then one needs an argument to support the adoption of that point of view rather than others, and it would beg the question to appeal to consequences to support that selection.

On the other hand, the objection could mean that, even though all the reasons, interpreted in a utilitarian sense, support one alternative, it is still possible to choose the other, because it is possible for one simply to follow one's emotions rather than any reasons. But if this is the objection, then, again,

24. Robert McKim and Peter Simpson, "On the Alleged Incoherence of Consequentialism," *New Scholasticism* 62 (1988): 351.

25. Joseph Boyle, Germain Grisez, and John Finnis, "Incoherence and Consequentialism (or Proportionalism)—A Rejoinder," *American Catholic Philosophical Quarterly* 64 (1990): 271–77.

the point it makes is true—and helpful—but does not destroy the argument. Our problematic choices are not between alternatives only one of which has reasons to support it while the others have only emotional appeal. Rather, in problematical choices there are reasons to support each alternative. That is, one does not need a moral theory to tell one not to act on emotion alone. A moral theory or norm is needed precisely to indicate why in most cases the reasons for a possible option are not morally compelling, or why these reasons rather than those should be acted upon. No one has claimed that no reasons at all can be given to support the practices of euthanasia, infanticide, or abortion. Rather, opponents of these practices must show that whatever reasons there are for such practices, they are not morally decisive, whereas the reasons against such practices are. Likewise, utilitarian defenders of abortion do not say that reasons cannot be given to support refraining from abortion, but—as utilitarians—that such reasons are outweighed by the reasons in support of abortion. It remains that in a morally problematical choice the options are incommensurable. It follows that utilitarianism does not provide a determinate standard by which to guide our actions, and so it cannot be appealed to in order to support the deliberate killing of an innocent person.

Finally, from this standpoint, one can see that utilitarianism, in effect, denies the intrinsic dignity of the human person. The easiest way to see this point is to think of a loved one. If my youngest son died, or was killed, this evil would not be merely the death of one human being. The death of my son would not be the same as any other death, since he is a unique person. His death, or even any other significant harm to him, would not be made up for by a benefit enjoyed by someone else. His life is unique and irreplaceable: if he died, no other child would replace him, and, by the same token, no good possessed by someone else can make up for, or equalize, a significant harm suffered by him. These points follow from the truth that the person is a unique and unrepeatable entity, of unique and irreplaceable value. Expressed otherwise—for this is not a descriptive proposition, but a moral one, an ought-proposition—we ought to care for each human being. And we see this truth, not perhaps when we argue about abstract or hypothetical cases presented in books about moral theory, but when we look at our children or our parents or our spouses. But utilitarianism can be applied only if the life of one person can be measured against the benefits possessed by others. Utilitarianism must proceed as if value or goodness were a single property, various amounts of which were instantiated in various places. Ultimately for utilitarianism, persons are valuable, not as unique, intrinsically valuable entities, but as potential components of a whole. But this view contradicts the truth we see when we understand that we ought to care for each person for his or her own sake. The choice to kill a child is a denial of the intrinsic dignity of human persons.

IV. The Argument that Abortion Is Sometimes Best for the Child

Sometimes it is argued in support of an abortion that the child who would result from the pregnancy would be unhappy anyway, and abortion would be better even for the child, so that the child's death is not really to be counted as bad. For example:

It is a low form of cruelty to insist ruthlessly on bringing into the world a child for whom there is no welcome, no proper care and nurture, and no chance for a decent life. It is all very well to argue about the rights of the fetus. But what about the rights of the child? There is no virtue in a legal insistence on one bringing into the world unwanted children doomed to poverty, disease and delinquency.[26]

26. Statement of C. Stanley Lowell, Americans United for Separation of Church and State, before the U.S. Senate, cited in James Burtchaell, *Rachel*

This argument claims, first, that one can judge that this baby's life would possess more unhappiness than happiness, and, second, that if one can confidently make such a judgment, then killing that baby is morally right. Both points, however, are problematical. First, it is far from clear that we are ever in a position to judge that a child's life will indeed contain more unhappiness than happiness.

Secondly, suppose one *could* judge that this baby's life would have more unhappiness than happiness in it. The question of how to evaluate that balance would still remain. Clearly, the argument assumes that either life is not intrinsically valuable, or a balance of suffering over enjoyment in a life overrides whatever value that life originally had. But although such a judgment may at times appeal to our emotions—as when someone is in excruciating pain—nevertheless, it could have rational appeal only if pleasant experience alone were intrinsically valuable. I argued against this position in chapter 2.[27] The baby's life is clearly that which has intrinsic value; hedonism is mistaken. And what is intrinsically valuable here cannot be outweighed by other basic human goods, since basic goods are incommensurable, and much less could it be outweighed by pains and sufferings.

v. Special Difficulties with Measuring the Consequences of Abortion

A. Problems in Measuring

I have argued that consequentialism cannot support the pro-abortion position because it is an unworkable theory. But I also

---

Weeping and Other Essays on Abortion (New York: Andrews and McMeel, 1982), 73.

27. There is an intelligible evil associated with pain, namely, the disintegration (or disharmony among different aspects of the self) it tends to bring about, but even this intelligible bad is incommensurable with death, and so it remains irrational to choose death to avoid such pain.

think that consequentialism's problems are especially acute in the case of abortion.

In order to say that killing an unborn child would produce better consequences than not killing him or her, one must, first, calculate (with some degree of probability) what the consequences of killing the child would be and what the consequences of not killing him or her would be, and, secondly, compare the two sets of consequences to one another, and be able to say that one set is objectively worse than the other.

Critics of consequentialism frequently point out the general difficulties in figuring out what the consequences of our actions would be—that is, how difficult it is to identify just what the total consequences will be, independent of the problem of how to measure them once identified. This problem is especially serious when one is considering whether a child is to be born or not. For to have an idea of what consequences his or her birth would have, in contrast to the consequences of killing him or her in the womb, one would have to know, or have a general idea of, what the consequences of all of the child's actions would be.

Suppose this person would perform five million actions throughout his or her life. Then, the general problem of not being able to discover all the consequences of these actions is multiplied considerably. It will not do to say that the remote consequences of one person's actions can be counted on to balance out. We know that good people can make a lasting difference for the good and bad people can make a lasting difference for the bad.

Suppose the relevant information by which to make one's decision *were* the overall goodness or badness of all of the consequences of one's actions. The point I wish to make is that it would be unreasonable to base such a crucial decision as to kill a person on such a minute fraction (the part that is known) of the total relevant information. When our information about the total consequences of births falls so short of the complete in-

formation about all of the consequences of complete lives, the
reasonable conclusion is that the total consequences cannot be
the basis on which we should make our decisions. We would
never have any certainty in these areas if the balance of good
over evil of the total consequences were the rational basis on
which to decide.

Moreover, it is especially clear in the case of abortion that
even if we could calculate what a good portion of the consequences would be, we still could not measure those consequences against one another. Suppose a woman already has five
children, is on welfare, and her husband has abandoned the
family. Would an abortion produce the least bad consequence
in that case? Proponents of abortion might argue that if she has
the baby, she would be unable to support it, and her other children would suffer even more than otherwise. If she has the
abortion, she could more easily get a job and support the family
she already has.

But one must also remember (1) the bad which consists in
the child's death, (2) the bad which consists in one's *choosing*
the child's death, (3) the emotional and psychological impact
such a choice might have on the mother making that choice,
(4) the emotional and psychological impact on other children
in the family,[28] and (5) the impact abortion has on society's at-
titudes toward other groups of unwanted people in society,
such as the elderly, the retarded, and the handicapped. All of
these are bad consequences of the choice to abort. Now, it is
difficult to see how one can measure these bads against the bad
consisting in the economic harm and the strain consequent
upon that economic harm. By what standard does one measure
these bads? If the woman already had six children, the youngest
a year old, how many would say that she should kill the one-

---

28. The knowledge that parents have aborted other babies can suggest to
children that their parents' love is conditional. On the impact which abortion
has on other children, see David Reardon, *Aborted Women: Silent No More*
(Chicago: Loyola University Press, 1987), 219–31.

year-old child? Would we say that *that* child's death was a lesser evil than the evils the family endures in living in bad conditions because of their poverty? By what criterion can we say that death is worse than poverty? By what criterion can we say that death, choosing death, and possibly living with profound guilt after choosing death, is less bad than poverty?

B. The Impact on the Mother

It is frequently treated as obvious that the bad consequences of having an abortion are rather minor for the mother. Abortion is presented as the solution to her problems, rather than as a source of new problems. But the possibility that having the abortion could result in terrible consequences for the mother is often ignored.

1. Physical Consequences for the Mother. There are possible physical complications from the abortion procedure. Some proponents of abortion claim that studies have shown that abortion is very safe.[29] But other studies show significantly high risks for various physical complications, such as a perforated uterus, infection due to an incomplete abortion, an incompetent cervix, and even death from internal hemorrhaging.[30]

It is difficult to say how much weight a utilitarian would have to give to considerations of physical harm. But one should note that the rate of complications for the abortion procedure is probably significantly higher than what is often stated. It has been argued that many of the sources for data on physical complications from abortions are derived from biased sources.[31]

29. E.g., D. A. Grimes and W. Cates, "Complications from Legally Induced Abortions," *American Journal of Obstetrics and Gynecology* 150 (1984): 689–94.

30. Cf. Frederick Taussig, "Effects of Abortion on General Health and Reproductive Function," *Child and Family* 20 (1988): 305–15; Reardon, *Aborted Women,* chap. 3; Thomas Hilgers, Dennis Horan, and David Mall, *New Perspectives on Human Abortion* (Frederick, Md.: University Publications of America, 1981), 92–123.

31. See Matthew J. Bulfin, M.D., "A New Problem in Adolescent Gyne-

Abortion is physically dangerous for the girl or woman contemplating it, and this danger is often simply ignored. If it is not ignored, it weakens the utilitarian case for abortion, since the potential harm counterbalances the perceived benefits of the abortion.

2. *The Psychological Impact on the Mother.* The psychological consequences for the mother are even more significant. Many psychiatrists and psychologists have identified a condition known as "post-abortion syndrome." This is an emotional and psychological condition caused by repressed grief and guilt about the abortion. In a book written to help women whose emotional lives have been seriously impaired by their experience of abortion, Nancy Michels lists some of the reactions as follows:

Depression, grief, anxiety, sadness, shame, helplessness, hopelessness, sorrow, lowered self-esteem, distrust, hostility toward self and others, regret, insomnia, recurring dreams, nightmares, anniversary reactions, suicidal behavior, alcohol and/or chemical dependencies, sexual dysfunction, insecurity, numbness, painful re-experiencing of the abortion, relationship disruption, communication impairment, isolation, fetal fantasies, self-condemnation, flash-back, uncontrollable weeping, eating disorders, preoccupation, distorted thinking, bitterness, and a sense of loss and emptiness.[32]

Here are some of the ways some women have described their emotional and psychological difficulties experienced after their abortions:

I started to think about my life then—something clicked in me. I began to realize that everything I had done—the abortions, drugs, affairs, depressions—had all been a result of the circumstances of

cology," *Southern Medical Journal* 72 (1979): 968; Burtchael, *Rachel Weeping*, 2; and Reardon, *Aborted Women*.

32. Nancy Michels, *Helping Women Recover from Abortion* (Minneapolis: Bethany House, 1988), 30–31.

my first abortion. After that, I couldn't make any decisions at all. I knew that all the sex and drugs were wrong, but my mind was so clouded with negatives that I wasn't in any position to get my life straightened out. . . .

It's amazing how you can think that you know all the answers, and that what you're doing is right and good. And then ten years down the road you look back at your actions, and you realize that you were just living a bunch of lies, and that each lie just seems to compound the other ones and force them deeper and deeper into my subconscious. It has taken me so long to admit and discuss this.[33]

In a letter written to the *Tampa Tribune,* a woman writes:

I am thirty-four, married seven years. I had an abortion not quite four years ago. The pain of the knowledge of what I did is permanent, deep and fresh again when I least expect it. A word about a child, Mother's Day, a song—can literally rip me apart. There is never any warning. In the middle of the happiest moments, something will trigger a sadness for my action.

I can't make you feel how I feel or how I felt. I would be writing for hours. Even if I talked to you, you could not know the pain I've set myself up for. It's not just babies that abortion kills. It's mothers too.[34]

It is difficult to say what percentage of women who have abortions experience such devastating psychological consequences. But several factors suggest that such experiences are widespread.

First, because of the shame involved, it is likely that many more women experience profound grief and guilt than openly admit to it. Second, many hide their grief and guilt even from themselves. Suppression of negative feelings about the abortion, rationalization, sometimes even intense activism in the pro-abortion cause have often been cited by women who later

33. Quoted in Reardon, *Aborted Women,* xx.
34. Quoted in Reardon, *Aborted Women,* 68.

regret their abortions as ways of trying to avoid facing up to the problem.[35]

Third, women who regret their abortions and who have experienced profound emotional or psychological problems have formed support groups. Among such groups are Women Exploited by Abortion (WEBA) and American Victims of Abortion. Each of these organizations has over a hundred local chapters and membership in the tens of thousands. The strength of such organizations suggests that serious problems are not atypical of the abortion experience.[36]

I am not arguing that one can present a cogent utilitarian case against abortion, for I have already tried to show that utilitarianism is unable to present a cogent case for any position. Rather, my point is that utilitarian arguments *for* abortion generally underestimate the harm done to the mother. In some cases the bad effects of not aborting are detailed and pondered, while the bad effects of aborting are simply ignored. When the possible bad effects on the mother are taken into account, it is easier to see that the utilitarian argument for abortion is unsound.

It also is important to make clear that the case against abortion is not motivated solely by concern for the well-being of the unborn human beings killed. It is not that abortion would be a great thing for women, but, since it is immoral, it must

35. For some examples, see Reardon, *Aborted Women,* 36–40, 73–80.

36. After recounting some stories of women from sources other than members of WEBA, David Reardon argues: "The trend is clear to anyone who looks. The negative, WEBA-like abortion experience is the rule rather than the exception. Many aborted women will deny it by hiding their emotions and telling little or nothing of their experience. Others may hide it behind the anger and bitterness they feel toward other persons who were involved, especially the male. But most will admit they are troubled; they simply don't know what else to do other than to try to forget it and move on" (Ibid., 69). See also Kathleen McDonnell, *Not an Easy Choice: A Feminist Re-examines Abortion* (Boston: South End Press, 1984).

be stopped. Rather, abortion harms women perhaps as much as it harms the unborn human beings it kills.

I conclude that because of the numerous difficulties facing utilitarianism itself, and also because many of these difficulties are especially serious in the application of utilitarianism to abortion, the utilitarian argument for abortion does not succeed.

Works Cited

Angelo, E. Joanne. "Psychiatric Sequelae of Abortion: The Many Faces of Post-Abortion Grief." *Linacre Quarterly* 59 (1992): 69–80.

Arey, Leslie Brainerd. *Developmental Anatomy.* 7th ed. Philadelphia: Saunders, 1974.

Ashley, Benedict. "Delayed Hominization: Catholic Theological Perspective." In *The Interaction of Catholic Bioethics and Secular Society.* Proceedings of the Eleventh Bishops' Workshop, Dallas, Tex., edited by Russell E. Smith, 163–79. Braintree, Mass.: Pope John Center, 1992.

———. "A Critique of the Theory of Delayed Hominization." In *An Ethical Evaluation of Fetal Experimentation: An Interdisciplinary Study,* edited by Donald McCarthy and Albert Moraczewski, 113–33. St. Louis: Pope John XXIII Medical-Moral Research and Education Center, 1976.

Ashley, Benedict, and Albert Moraczewski. "Is the Biological Subject of Human Rights Present from Conception?" In *The Fetal Tissue Issue: Medical and Ethical Aspects,* edited by Peter Cataldo and Albert Moraczewski, 33–60. Braintree, Mass.: Pope John Center, 1994.

Austin, C. R. *Human Embryos: The Debate on Assisted Reproduction.* Oxford: Oxford University Press, 1989.

Barry, Robert. "Thomson and Abortion." In *Abortion: A New Generation of Catholic Responses,* edited by Stephen J. Heaney, 163–76. Braintree, Mass.: Pope John Center, 1992.

Beckwith, Francis J. "Personal Bodily Rights, Abortion, and Unplugging the Violinist." *International Philosophical Quarterly* 32 (1992): 105–18.

Bedate, C. A., and R. C. Cefalo. "The Zygote: To Be or Not to Be a Person." *Journal of Medicine and Philosophy* 14 (1989): 641–45.

Benn, S. I. "Abortion, Infanticide, and Respect for Persons." In Feinberg, *The Problem of Abortion*, 135–44.

Bigelow, John, and Robert Pargetter. "Morality, Potential Persons and Abortion." *American Philosophical Quarterly* 25 (1988): 173–81.

Bole, Thomas. "Metaphysical Accounts of the Zygote as a Person." *Journal of Medicine and Philosophy* 14 (1989): 647–53.

Bonvoglia, Angela, ed. *The Choices We Made: Twenty-Five Women Speak Out About Abortion.* New York: Random House, 1991.

Bolton, Martha Brandt. "Responsible Women and Abortion Decisions." In *Having Children: Philosophical and Legal Reflections on Parenthood,* edited by Onora O'Neill and William Ruddick, 39–51. New York: Oxford University Press, 1979.

Boyle, Joseph M., and Thomas D. Sullivan. "The Diffusiveness of the Intention Principle: A Counter-Example." *Philosophical Studies* 31 (1977): 357–60.

Boyle, Joseph, Germain Grisez, and John Finnis. "Incoherence and Consequentialism (or Proportionalism)—A Rejoinder." *American Catholic Philosophical Quarterly* 64 (1990): 271–77.

Braine, David. *The Human Person: Animal and Spirit.* Notre Dame: University of Notre Dame Press, 1992.

Brody, Baruch. *Abortion and the Sanctity of Human Life: A Philosophical View.* Cambridge: MIT Press, 1975.

Bulfin, Matthew J., M.D. "A New Problem in Adolescent Gynecology." *Southern Medical Journal* 72 (1979): 968.

Burtchaell, James. *Rachel Weeping and Other Essays on Abortion.* New York: Andrews and McMeel, 1982.

Campbell, John, and Robert Pargetter. "Goodness and Fragility." *American Philosophical Quarterly* 23 (1986): 155–65.

Carter, W. R. *The Elements of Metaphysics.* New York: McGraw-Hill, 1990.

Cranford, Ronald. "The Persistent Vegetative State: The Medical Reality (Getting the Facts Straight)." *Hastings Center Report* 18 (1988): 27–28.

Daly, T. V. "Identifiying the Origin of a Human Life: The Search for a Marker Event for the Origin of Human Life." *St. Vincent's Bioethics Center Newsletter,* no. 1 (March 1987): 14–16.

———. "Individuals, Syngamy, and the Origin of Human Life: A Reply to Buckle and Dawson." *St. Vincent's Bioethics Center Newsletter,* 6, no. 4 (December 1988): 1–7.

Davis, Michael. "Foetuses, Famous Violinists, and the Right to Continued Aid." *Philosophical Quarterly* 33 (1983): 259–78.

de Dorlodot, Henri. "A Vindication of the Mediate Animation Theory." In *Theology and Evolution,* edited by E. C. Messenger, 259–83. London: Sands and Co., 1949.

Devine, Philip E. "The Moral Basis of Vegetarianism." In *Moral Dilemmas:*

Readings in Ethics and Social Philosophy, edited by Richard C. Purtill, 389–407. Belmont, Cal.: Wadsworth, 1985.

Donceel, Joseph. "Immediate Animation and Delayed Hominization." *Theological Studies* 31 (1970): 76–105.

Dworkin, Ronald. *Life's Dominion: An Argument About Abortion, Euthanasia, and Individual Freedom.* New York: Knopf, 1993.

Englehardt, H. Tristram, Jr. "The Ontology of Abortion." *Ethics* 84 (1973–74): 217–34.

English, Jane. "Abortion and the Concept of a Person." In Feinberg, *The Problem of Abortion,* 151–60. First published in *Canadian Journal of Philosophy* 5 (1975): 233–43.

Ervin, Paula. *Women Exploited: The Other Victims of Abortion.* Huntington, Ind.: Our Sunday Visitor, 1985.

Feinberg, Joel, ed. *The Problem of Abortion.* 2d ed. Belmont, Cal.: Wadsworth, 1984.

Finnis, John. *Natural Law and Natural Rights.* Oxford: Clarendon Press, 1980.

Fisher, Anthony. "'When Did I Begin?' Revisited." *Linacre Quarterly* 58 (1991): 59–68.

Flannery, Kevin. "What is Included in a Means to an End." *Gregorianum* 74 (1993): 499–513.

Ford, Norman. *When Did I Begin?* New York: Cambridge University Press, 1988.

Frankena, William. *Ethics.* Englewood Cliffs, N.J.: Prentice-Hall, 1973.

Gerber, Rudolph. "When Is the Human Soul Infused?" *Laval théologique et philosophique* 22 (1966): 234–47.

Gillespie, Norman. "Abortion and Human Rights." In Feinberg, *The Problem of Abortion,* 94–101.

Grimes, D. A., and W. Cates. "Complications from Legally Induced Abortions." *Journal of Obstetrics and Gynecology* 150 (1984): 689–94.

Grisez, Germain. "Against Consequentialism." *American Journal of Jurisprudence* 23 (1978): 21–72.

———. "When Do People Begin?" *Proceedings of the American Catholic Philosophical Association* 63 (1990): 27–47.

Grisez, Germain, and Joseph Boyle. *Life and Death with Liberty and Justice.* Notre Dame: University of Notre Dame Press, 1978.

Grisez, Germain, Joseph Boyle, and John Finnis. *Nuclear Deterrence, Morality and Realism.* New York: Oxford University Press, 1987.

———. "Practical Principles, Moral Truth, and Ultimate Ends." *American Journal of Jurisprudence* 32 (1987): 99–151.

Grisez, Germain, and Russell Shaw. *Beyond the New Morality.* 3d ed. Notre Dame: University of Notre Dame Press, 1988.

Grobstein, Clifford. *Science and the Unborn.* New York: Basic Books, 1988.

Hallett, Garth. "The 'Incommensurability' of Values." *Heythrop Journal* 28 (1987): 373–87.

Hardin, Russell. *Morality Within the Limits of Reason.* Chicago: University of Chicago Press, 1988.

Heaney, Stephen J. "Aquinas and the Presence of the Human Embryo." *The Thomist* 56 (1992): 19–48.

Hilgers, Thomas, Dennis Horan, and David Mall. *New Perspectives on Human Abortion*. Frederick, Md.: University Publications of America, 1981.

Hursthouse, Rosalind. *Beginning Lives*. New York: Oxford University Press, 1988.

John Paul II. *Evangelium Vitae* (The Gospel of Life). Boston: St. Paul Books and Media, 1995.

Kamm, F. M. *Creation and Abortion: A Study in Moral and Legal Philosophy*. New York: Oxford University Press, 1992.

Kluge, Eike-Henner W. *The Practice of Death*. New Haven: Yale University Press, 1975.

Larsen, William J. *Human Embryology*. New York: Churchill Livingstone, 1993.

Lejeune, Jerome. *The Concentration Can: When Does Human Life Begin?* San Francisco: Ignatius Press, 1992.

Lonergan, Bernard. *Insight*. New York: Philosophical Library, 1970.

Mahkorn, Sandra Kathleen, and William Dolan. "Pregnancy and Sexual Assault." In Hilgers, Horan, and Mall, *New Perspectives on Human Abortion*, 182–98.

Marquis, Don. "Why Abortion is Immoral." *Journal of Philosophy* 86 (1989): 183–202.

McCloskey, H. J. "An Examination of Restricted Utilitarianism." In *Studies in Utilitarianism*, edited by Thomas K. Hearn, 231–51. New York: Appleton-Century-Crofts, 1971.

McDonnell, Kathleen. *Not an Easy Choice: A Feminist Re-examines Abortion*. Boston: South End Press, 1984.

McInerney, Peter. "Does a Fetus Already Have a Future-Like-Ours?" *Journal of Philosophy* 87 (1990): 264–68.

McKim, Robert, and Peter Simpson. "On the Alleged Incoherence of Consequentialism." *New Scholasticism* 62 (1988): 349–52.

McLaren, Anne. "The Embryo." In *Reproduction in Mammals*, 1–42. Bk. 2 of *Embryonic and Fetal Development*, edited by C. R. Austin and R. V. Short. 2d ed. Cambridge: Cambridge University Press, 1982.

Merleau-Ponty, Maurice. *The Phenomenology of Perception*. Translated by Colin Smith. New York: Routledge and Kegan Paul, 1962.

Michels, Nancy. *Helping Women Recover from Abortion*. Minneapolis: Bethany House, 1988.

Moore, Keith L. *Before We Are Born*, 2d ed. Philadelphia: Saunders, 1983.

Moraczewski, Albert. "Personhood: Entry and Exit." In *The Twenty-Fifth Anniversary of Vatican II: A Look Back and a Look Ahead*. Proceedings of the Ninth Bishops' Workshop, Dallas, Tex., edited by Russell E. Smith, 78–101. Braintree, Mass.: Pope John Center, 1990.

Munson, Ronald. *Intervention and Reflection: Basic Issues in Medical Ethics*. 4th ed. Belmont, Cal.: Wadsworth, 1992.

Ney, G. "Mental Health and Abortion: Review and Analysis." *Psychiatric Journal of the University of Ottawa* 14 (1989): 513–15.

Noonan, John. "How to Argue About Abortion." In *Morality in Practice,* edited by James Sterba, 149–58. 2d ed. Belmont, Cal.: Wadsworth, 1988.

Nozick, Robert. *Anarchy, State and Utopia.* New York: Basic Books, 1974.

———. *Philosophical Explanation.* Cambridge: Harvard University Press, 1981.

O'Rahilly, Ronan, and Fabiola Mueller. *Developmental Stages in Human Embryos.* Washington, D.C.: Carnegie Institute of Washington, 1987.

Parfit, Derek. *Reasons and Persons.* Oxford: Oxford University Press, 1984.

Purdy, Laura, and Michael Tooley. "Is Abortion Murder?" In *Abortion Pro and Con,* edited by Robert Perkins, 129–49. Cambridge, Mass.: Schlenkman, 1974.

Quinn, Warren. "Abortion: Identity and Loss." *Philosophy and Public Affairs* 13 (1984): 24–54.

Reardon, David. *Aborted Women: Silent No More.* Chicago: Loyola University Press, 1987.

Russell, Bertrand. *The Philosophy of Logical Atomism.* Edited by David Pears. La Salle, Ill.: Open Court, 1985.

Schwarz, Stephen. *The Moral Question of Abortion.* Chicago: Loyola University Press, 1990.

Shannon, Thomas, and Allan Wolter. "Reflections on the Moral Status of the Pre-Embryo." *Theological Studies* 51 (1990): 603–26.

Smart, J. J. C., and B. A. O. Williams. *Utilitarianism: For and Against.* Cambridge: Cambridge University Press, 1973.

Sommers, Mary Catherine. "Living Together: Burdensome Pregnancy and the Hospitable Self." In *Catholicism and Abortion,* edited by Stephen Heaney, 243–64. Braintree, Mass.: Pope John Center, 1992.

Steinbock, Bonnie. *Life Before Birth: The Moral and Legal Status of Embryos and Fetuses.* New York: Oxford University Press, 1992.

Suarez, Antoine. "Hydatidiform Moles and Teratomas Confirm the Human Identity of the Preimplantation Embryo." *Journal of Medicine and Philosophy* 15 (1990): 627–35.

Sumner, L. W. *Abortion and Moral Theory.* Princeton: Princeton University Press, 1981.

———. "A Third Way." In Feinberg, *The Problem of Abortion,* 71–93.

Swinburne, Richard. *The Evolution of the Soul.* Oxford: Clarendon Press, 1986.

Taussig, Frederick. "Effects of Abortion on General Health and Reproductive Function." *Child and Family* 20 (1988): 305–15.

Thomas Aquinas, Saint. *Summa contra gentiles.* 2 vols. Madrid: Biblioteca Autores Cristianos, 1968.

———. *Summa theologiae.* 5 vols. Madrid: Biblioteca Autores Cristianos, 1963.

Thomson, Judith Jarvis. "A Defense of Abortion." In Feinberg, *The Problem of Abortion,* 173–87. First published in *Philosophy and Public Affairs* 1 (1971): 47–66.

———. "Rights and Deaths." In *Rights, Restitution, and Risk,* edited by William Parent, 20–32. Cambridge: Harvard University Press, 1986.

Tischler, C. L. "Adolescent Suicide Attempts Following Elective Abortion: A Special Case of Anniversary Reaction." *Pediatrics* 68 (1990): 670–71.

Tooley, Michael. "Abortion and Infanticide." In *Rights and Wrongs of Abortion,* edited by Marshall Cohen, Thomas Nagel, and Thomas Scanlon, xx–xx. Princeton: Princeton University Press, 1974. First published in *Philosophy and Public Affairs* 2 (1972): 37–65.

———. *Abortion and Infanticide.* New York: Oxford University Press, 1983.

Van De Veer, Donald. "Justifying 'Wholesale Slaughter.'" In Feinberg, *The Problem of Abortion,* 65–70.

Vatican Council II. *The Constitution on the Church in the Modern World (Gaudium et Spes).* Edited by Austin Flannery. Northport, N. Y.: Costello, 1975.

Wade, Francis C. "Potentiality in the Abortion Discussion." *Review of Metaphysics* 29 (1975): 239–55.

Warren, Mary Ann. "On the Moral and Legal Status of Abortion." In Feinberg, *The Problem of Abortion,* 102–19.

Werner, Richard. "Abortion: The Ontological and Moral Status of the Unborn." *Social Theory and Practice* 3 (1974): 201–20.

Wertheimer, Roger. "Understanding the Abortion Argument." In Feinberg, *The Problem of Abortion,* 43–57. First published in *Philosophy and Public Affairs* 2 (1972): 67–95.

Wreen, Michael. "Abortion and Pregnancy Due to Rape." *Philosophia* 21 (1992): 201–20.

ovum, 3, 5, 70, 71, 76, 90, 91, 102, 103

parents, 119, 139
Parfit, Derek, 40
Pargetter, Robert, 134, 140
perceiving, 34
perforated uterus, 152
person, 5, 6, 7–45; defined, 59
personal identity, 18, 32
personality, 33, 44
personhood, 8, 61
pets, 119
physical behavior, 111, 112, 114
physical consequences of abortion, 151–53
Pope John Paul II, 116
positional differences, 97
post-abortion syndrome, 153
potentiality, 18, 76, 79; active and passive, 24–29; immediately exercisable, 23; *also see* capacity
poverty, 151
preference utilitarianism, 133
pregnancy due to rape, 108, 120–24, 127
prejudice, 64–68
primary organizer, 77
primitive streak, 77, 89, 90
psychological consequences of abortion, 151, 153–56
psychological continuity, 29–31, 38–43
psychological traits, 11, 18
public policy, 1
Purdy, Laura, 11, 13, 14, 19, 20, 21

quickening, 73
Quinn, Warren, 22

rabbits, 35, 36, 41, 83
Rahner, Karl, 88
rape, 108, 112, 120–24
Reardon, David, 123, 153, 154, 155, 156
reasons for acting, 53
recombination, 90
religion, 68
reproduction, 84
reprogramming, 33
responsibility, 108, 109, 110, 111, 118, 119, 121, 126
right to life, 7, 17, 18, 43, 106

rights, 7, 10–12, 15–16,
RNA, 98
Roe v Wade, 71, 73
RU-486, 76
Russell, Bertrand, 37, 38

Schoonenberg, Piet, 90
Schwarz, Stephan, 129
science fiction, 78, 79
self, 12, 18
self-consciousness, 12, 14, 20, 22, 23, 32, 33, 37
self-esteem, 123
selfishness, 146
semen, 85
sensation, 34, 35
sentience, 48, 50–54, 58
sex, 128
sex cells, 70
sexual desire, 50
sexual intercourse, 117, 118
Shannon, Thomas, 79–90, 92–98, 104
Shaw, Russell, 51, 52
sheriff, 137
Short, R. V., 96
side effects, 108, 110, 111, 112, 113, 114, 115, 117, 118, 135, 139
Simpson, Peter, 145, 146
slave, 16, 17, 20, 21, 30, 60
sleeping persons, 19, 20, 22
slippery slope argument, 8
Smart, J. J. C., 137
Sommers, Mary Catherine, 123
soul, 80
species, 9, 70, 71, 76, 82, 97
specific difference, 81
sperm, 3, 27, 28, 99, 102
spontaneous generation, 87
Steinbock, Bonnie, 47
Suarez, Antoine, 5, 99, 100
substance, 41, 56, 58, 71
Sullivan, Thomas, 114
Sumner, L. W., 47–67
Swinburne, Richard, 35
synapses, 76
syngamy, 3

Taussig, Frederick, 152
theology, 103
Thomas Aquinas, 79–90, 91, 114
Thomson, Judith Jarvis, 2, 105–30

Index

accidental properties, 74, 76
acorn, 71
active potentiality, 92
adoption, 109, 115, 117, 121
adults, 48, 50, 56
affections, 50
affirmation, 34
agent, 35, 41, 43
aggregate, 93
aggression, 50
aggressor, 105, 129–30
American Victims of Abortion, 155
Americans United for Separation of Church and State, 148
amoeba, 71
analogy, 141
androgenetic eggs, 100
Angelo, E. Joanne, 123
animals, 35, 41, 48, 50, 59, 60
Arey, Leslie Brainerd, 70
Aristotle, 28, 58, 71
Ashley, Benedict, 85, 86, 98, 101
Austin, C. R., 96, 97
autonomy, 30–31, 123

Barry, Robert, 113

basic goods, 133, 138–40, 144, 149
Beckwith, Francis J., 118
Bedate, C. A., 98, 99, 100
benevolence, 146
Benn, S. I., 47
Bigelow, John, 134
biological relationship, 108, 122
biologists, 69, 70
birth, 7–45, 74, 89
blastocyst, 94, 95, 96, 98
body-soul, 31–37
body-swapping, 39–43
Bole, Thomas, 99, 100
Bolton, Martha Brandt, 105
Bonvoglia, Angela, 132
Boyle, Joseph M., 30, 54, 56, 58, 111, 114, 139, 146
brain, 75, 76, 78, 89, 102, 137, 138
brain-death, 75, 79
Braine, David, 36
Brody, Baruch, 74–79, 129
Bulfin, Matthew J., 152
burdens, 108, 121, 122, 128
Burtchaell, James, 123, 153
butterfly, 84

calculation of consequences, 150
Campbell, John, 140
capacity, 5, 20; *also see* potentiality
capital punishment, 132
careers, 117
Carter, W. R., 40
Cates, W., 152
Cefalo, R. C., 98, 99, 100
cells, 70, 93, 95
cerebral cortex, 81, 82
child abandonment, 109
chimpanzee, 18, 19, 49
Christian, 144
chromosomes, 72
cigarette smoking, 116, 117, 118
clock mechanism, 96
cloning, 93
cockroach, 50
coma, 5, 12, 14, 19, 20, 22, 23, 26, 31–32
compaction, 97
conception, 3, 4, 6
concepts, 20
consciousness, 2, 17, 18, 33–37, 52
consequentialism, 131–56
contraception, 47
Cranford, Ronald, 23
criterion of moral standing, 48–68
criterion of personhood, 58–62

Daly, T. V., 3, 93
Davis, Michael, 122, 125, 128
de Dorlodot, Henri, 82
death, 125–26, 151
degrees of personhood, 46–68
delayed animation, 87
delayed hominization, 87, 88
derivative objection to abortion, 62–68
Descartes, Rene, 35
desires, 12, 14–20, 32
detached objection to abortion, 62–68
deus ex machina, 88
dignity, 55; of human person, 147, 148
direct killing, 113
distribution of goods, 133
DNA, 71, 92
dogs, 35, 36, 41, 83
Dolan, William, 123
dolphins, 49
Donceel, Joseph, 79–90
drunk drivers, 119

dualism, 31–37
duties, 49
Dworkin, Ronald, 62–68

ears, 35
education, 139
effect of abortion on other children, 151
ego, 34, 37, 43
egoism, 56
embryologists, 70, 102
embryology, 70, 88, 97
emotional distress, 121
emotional effects of abortion, 124, 151
emotions, 50, 147, 149
end and means, 111, 112, 114
Englehardt, H. Tristram, 22
English, Jane, 10
Ervin, Paula, 123
essential properties, 77
essentialism, 74
experience-machine, 51, 56
experiences, 14, 17, 31, 32, 37–43
eyes, 35

fairness, 118, 121
fathers, 118, 120
Feinberg, Joel, 16
fertilization, 3, 70, 71, 99, 102, 103, 104
fetal experimentation, 76
Finnis, John, 56, 110, 135, 139, 146
Fisher, Anthony, 95
Flannery, Kevin, 113
flourishing, 143
Ford, Norman, 70–100, 102
Frankenstein, 66
freedom, 5
fulfillment, 53, 56, 142
future generations, 14, 20, 21

gastrulation, 90, 91
genes, 3, 4
genetic material, 27, 100
genetic structure, 4, 9, 72, 96
geneticist, 72
Gerber, Rudolph, 84
gestation, 46–68
Gewirth, Alan, 57, 58
Gillespie, Norman, 47, 57
goal-directedness, 96
God, 60, 86, 88, 103, 104, 144
good, 53, 55, 56, 141–43

gradualist position, 47–68
greater good, lesser evil, 144
grief, 154–55
Grimes, D. A. 152
Grisez, Germain, 30, 89, 90, 111, 139, 141, 145, 146
Grobstein, Clifford, 92, 94

habitus, 28
Hallet, Garth, 140, 141
handicapped, 151
happiness, 134, 135, 136, 143, 149
Hardin, Russell, 137
Heaney, Stephen J., 86
heart condition, 112
hedonism, 51
hedonistic utilitarianism, 133
hemorrhaging, 152
Hilgers, Thomas, 123, 152
homicide, 76
Horan, Dennis, 123, 152
human beings, 144
human fulfillment, 133
Hume, David, 37
Hursthouse, Rosalind, 128
hydatidiform mole, 5, 72, 99, 100, 101–2, 103
hylomorphism, 79–90

ideal utilitarianism, 133
impartiality, 146
implantation, 95
incommensurability of options for choice, 138–48
incomplete abortions, 152
individual, 71, 90, 91, 94
individuality, 69
infant mortality, 104
infants, 16, 17, 18, 22
infection, 152
innocent person, 1, 105, 112, 121, 122
intentional killing, 1, 2, 105, 107, 110, 111, 112, 113, 115, 131
interests, 15, 16, 17, 32, 33, 48, 52
intrinsic goods, 133, 139, 140

James, William, 37
judgment, 34
justice, 121, 124, 128, 130, 136–38

Kamm, F. M., 106, 125–26

kidney donation, 111
killing in self-defense, 114
Kluge, Eike-Henner, 23

Larsen, William J., 70
legality, 1
Lejeune, Jerome, 72, 93
life, 124
living things, 24
Lonergan, Bernard, 84
Lowell, C. Stanley, 148

Mahkorn, Sandra Kathleen, 123
Mall, David, 123, 152
Marquis, Don, 22
matter and form, 79–90
maximizing goods, 134
McCloskey, H. J., 136, 137
McDonnell, Kathleen, 123, 155
McKim, Robert, 145, 146
McLaren, Anne, 96
memory, 18, 30, 32, 33
mental states, 12, 14, 19, 22–29, 33, 34
mentally retarded, 54
Merlau-Ponty, Maurice, 36
Michels, Nancy, 123, 153
Moore, Keith, 70
Moraczewski, Albert, 85, 97, 98, 101
morning-after pills, 76
morula, 4
mother's life, 115
mother's right to choose, 106
Mueller, Fabiola, 70
Munson, Robert, 137, 138

natural kind, 75
neurons, 35, 76, 89
newborn, 89
Ney, G., 123
no-person argument, 7–45
no-subject view, 37–45
nonintentional killing, 105–30
Noonan, John, 120
Nozick, Robert, 26, 51, 52

O'Neill, Onora, 106
O'Rahilly, Ronan, 70
options, 52
organism, 5, 6, 11, 12, 14, 17, 27, 33, 35–37, 43, 44, 56, 71, 76, 77, 79, 8, 89, 92, 95, 102

Tischler, C. L., 123
Tooley, Michael, 7–45, 88
totipotency, 95, 97
twinning, 90–102

ultimate reasons for acting, 59
understanding, 34, 35
unhappiness, 149
United States Supreme Court, 71
utilitarianism, 131–56

value, 140–43
Van De Veer, Donald, 8, 9
Vatican Council II, 144
viability, 71–74
violence, 121

violinist, 107–11, 128

Wade, Francis, 24
Warren, Mary Ann, 9, 10, 11
wastage, 102–4
WEBA (Women Exploited by Abortion), 155
welfare, 134, 135, 136
Werner, Richard, 73
Wertheimer, Roger, 8
Williams, B. A. O., 137
Wolter, Allan, 79–90, 92–98, 104
Wreen, Michael, 128

zygote, 3, 4, 9, 27, 28, 70, 71, 76, 91, 92, 97, 99, 100

Abortion and Unborn Human Life was composed in Bembo by Brevis Press, Bethany, Connecticut; printed on 60-pound Booktext Natural and bound by BookCrafters, Chelsea, Michigan; and designed and produced by Kachergis Book Design, Pittsboro, North Carolina.